STRATEGY

BEYOND THE

HOCKEY STICK

STRATEGY

BEYOND THE

HOCKEY STICK

PEOPLE, PROBABILITIES, *and*

BIG MOVES *to* BEAT THE ODDS

CHRIS BRADLEY | MARTIN HIRT | SVEN SMIT

McKINSEY & COMPANY

For general information on our other products and services or for technical support, please contact our Customer Care Department within the United States at (800) 762-2974, outside the United States at (317) 572-3993, or fax (317) 572-4002.

Wiley publishes in a variety of print and electronic formats and by print-on-demand. Some material included with standard print versions of this book may not be included in e-books or in print-on-demand. If this book refers to media such as a CD or DVD that is not included in the version you purchased, you may download this material at http://booksupport.wiley.com. For more information about Wiley products, visit www.wiley.com.

ISBN 978-1-119-48762-3 (Hardcover)
ISBN 978-1-119-48763-0 (ePDF)
ISBN 978-1-119-48760-9 (ePub)

Printed in the United States of America.

10 9 8 7 6 5 4 3 2 1

To

Bini, Walter, and Hildegund Hirt

Bibi, Jan-Ferdel, and Ute Smit

Mel, Olivia, Alice, and Harriet Bradley

And to our

Partners and Colleagues at McKinsey & Company

for giving us the opportunity to beat the odds.

Contents

Introduction

Welcome to the strategy room

In the strategy room, human bias and social dynamics can prevent the necessary big moves from getting on the table, let alone getting executed. In this book we arm ourselves with hard data from thousands of companies to take the "social side of strategy" head on.

I sn't there another way?"

We hear that all the time, and you must have asked yourself that question, too—probably more than once. Perhaps after an exhausting marathon of strategy sessions that are supposed to be discussions but really are just presentations. Perhaps after feeling compelled to say "yes" to another investment proposal with uncertain prospects. Perhaps after one of the usual discussions to re-allocate resources to growth opportunities that go nowhere.

Over decades of working with hundreds of the most senior business leaders around the world, we agreed:

"There has to be another way . . ."

Books about improving the strategy process fill our shelves, packed with frameworks and anecdotes that claim to crack the code of successful strategy.[1] As interesting as these books are to read, as inspiring as their case examples are, it seems we are still short a breakthrough. Today's strategic challenges are, in fact, very similar to what they've been over the ages, despite the serious efforts of a lot of smart people.

This book belongs on a different shelf. Rather than relying on the traditional approach of best practices and inspiring anecdotes, we use broad and deep empirical research. We have identified a small number of performance levers that, according to the factual evidence we compiled—and our experience in implementing them—can be used to greatly increase your odds of success. We believe we've also found the one—often overlooked—factor responsible for many of the conundrums facing us in the strategy room, the one factor that has perplexed generations of business leaders, the factor that causes so many strategies to not work out as planned. That factor is what we call the social side of strategy.

In this book, we use empirical insights to finally help you and other business leaders chart a course to address the social side of strategy and, as a result, develop better, bigger, bolder strategies.

There *is* another way!

You are not alone

As we begin our journey together through the empirics and the social side of strategy, let's peer into the strategy room and look at some of the scenes playing out there. These scenes probably feel familiar to you because they are surprisingly common despite all those books and articles about how to get to better strategy, better decisions, and better business performance.

As the strategy process starts, the team agrees that this year you will avoid huge documents with 150 slides and endless appendices. You commit to having real conversations about the future of the business and the tough choices you'll have to make. Then, two days before the first meeting, three of those 150-page documents land in the CEO's in-box with a thud. So much for real conversations. You are back wading through details in carefully scripted presentations that numb the senses before anybody has a chance to fully grasp the content.

Or, you decide that you need to have a deep strategic rethink after a stretch of indifferent results. The top team agrees on a change in direction. The board approves. Then the CFO takes over and turns that vision into a first-year budget. The boldness oozes away as those who stand to lose resources mount rear-guard actions and as other immune responses to real changes kick in. Somehow, that bold rethink produces a new budget that looks a lot like last year's budget. It's back to business as usual.

How about a third scenario? The strategy is agreed on. It all looks good on paper, and there is loads of compelling backup. But, somehow, deep down, everybody senses that the strategy is nothing more than hopeful thinking. It is a little too kind to the egos of the people who made it and a little too unwilling to embrace the harsh reality of competition. People two or three levels down in the organization—the ones who engage with actual customers, the ones who often weren't really part of the strategy process—conclude that management is stuck in a bubble, roll their eyes, and just get on with what they were doing. All that "new" strategy ends up being good for is justifying some uneconomic projects—the ones labeled "strategic" because they lose money; everybody knows that no real change in trajectory will happen because of them.

Even if you are the CEO, it can feel at times as if the inertia caused by individual behaviors and social dynamics is rather hard to deal with—and getting in the way of doing the right thing for your business. One of our client CEOs in Australia recently reflected: "I am well aware of the fact that we should be moving faster in that direction, but I have to bring the team along."

You might be in the enviable position of leading an agile start-up or an amazing, Amazon-scale institution that still operates like it did on Day 1. If so, congratulations. You may find some of the empirics in this book interesting because of what they show about what works and what doesn't in strategies, but you should really just keep doing what you're doing. If you are like the managers we more commonly come across, however, you will easily recognize the symptoms we are talking about and be keen to confront the social side of strategy. And even if you are Amazon-like, you might use some of the insights shared here to see a slip coming ahead of time.

The villain is the social side of strategy

We all know that we go into the strategy process loaded with individual and institutional biases and that group dynamics in the strategy room often distort results. But that's where the thinking about social dynamics usually ends. How often are we making an explicit effort to understand these factors and to properly deal with them? Don't we tend to shrug our shoulders and soldier on? Too often, we seem to pretend that the strategy process is just about solving an analytical problem, knowing deep down that the analysis is really the easy part.

Frameworks and tools, the likes of which you find in your typical business book or consulting deck, can be useful in structuring your thinking and can help generate ideas. Unfortunately, they usually don't help us break through the real barriers to good strategy. The simple reason: The social side of strategy can overwhelm the intellectual side.

"Collins, it's been brought to my attention
that your secret institutional biases are in
direct conflict with mine."

Peter Drucker famously said that "Culture eats strategy for breakfast."[2] Nowhere is that more evident than in the strategy room. How
can that be? After all, that room is full of smart and experienced people who welcome an intellectual challenge. But strategy isn't the only
thing that's at stake here. Jobs—even careers—are on the line, too. You
can lose your job or status if you overpromise or under-deliver on your
performance goals. So, not surprisingly, caution reigns—and a strategy
process that is about job protection rarely produces the best outcomes
for the company. The budget process intrudes, too. You may be discussing a 5-year strategy, but everyone knows that what really matters is
the first-year budget. Inevitably, other sorts of games are played. Most
managers, for instance, will try to secure resources for the coming year
while deferring accountability for the returns on these investments as
far as possible into the future—maybe even long enough that people
will have forgotten about the original commitments, or that they
themselves will have moved on to the next position. Even the most
successful business leaders are human, after all.

The strategy room is full of so many competing agendas and social
games that you might have sometimes wondered why people spent so
much time and effort on the analysis and presentation preparations in
the first place.

The outcome of all these dynamics is the hockey stick, confidently
showing future success after the all-too-familiar dip on next year's

budget. Truly, if ever there was one, the hockey stick is the icon of the strategy process. If we just mention the phrase, we get a knowing glance and a wry smile from the executives we've shared our research with.

With this book, we want to break the hockey stick. We want to address the social side of strategy, so the big moves that drive economic profit and shareholder value can actually happen.

Where is the outside view?

For more than 5 years now, the three of us have invested in understanding why things get bogged down so easily in the strategy process and on developing a new angle on how to deal with the issues. Having spent decades consulting with hundreds of companies across the globe, and having seen countless strategic plans, we began this journey by drawing on our personal observations. But we also decided to take our own medicine: We have tried to push past the usual anecdotes and juxtaposed experience with the reality of hard facts on corporate performance. We supplemented our observations with detailed research and analysis of several thousand of the world's largest companies. These are big-sample empirics—not the traditional collection of a few dozen, interview-based case studies.

We found that in most strategy rooms there simply aren't enough data, and certainly not all the right data. That may seem to be an odd statement, given our complaints about all those 150-page documents and their endless appendices. But those documents tend to take too narrow a view of the world. They are based on an "inside view"—the data from your own industry, the perspective of your own company, and the experience of your own team and of the executives in the strategy room.[3] The materials in strategy rooms today provide detail, but no reference data with predictive power. Interestingly, the more detailed the information you have, the more you lead yourself to believe that you know; and the more your confidence grows, the higher the risk of arriving at the wrong conclusions.[4]

When changing times demand a really big shift in strategy, this inside view turns out to be even more of a problem. It's an inside view of the wrong world, and you are caught blindsided.

"He's been brought in to give us the ultimate
out-of-the-room perspective."

Rather than an ever-more-precise inside view, strategy needs an "outside view," where data about the thousands of other experiences by other executives and their companies in other strategy rooms are brought into your own strategy room to shape the discussion. Why benchmark just your operational KPIs when you could have an equally compelling, objective reference point for your strategy? Why not calibrate how good your strategy really is against a broad set of comparative data?

The problem, you might say, is that every situation is unique, right? "No other company has our brand, our resources, our set of competitors, our customers, our challenges, our opportunities." And companies aren't exactly sharing all their data with the world to make it easy for you to compare yourself against them, anyway. Well, yes. That's why there never has been a comprehensive database of strategic success and failure—until now.

We looked at publicly available information on dozens of variables for thousands of companies and found a manageable number of levers—10, in fact—that explain over 80 percent of up-drift and down-drift in corporate performance.[5]

We'll share those data with you in this book, to give you that "outside view." We will show you a way to see how your strategy stacks up—before you ever leave the strategy room, and before you start to execute your strategy. If you don't think you've given yourself strong enough odds of success, you can fall back, regroup, and reformulate your strategy to improve your chances. All that, before you start down a costly road that might just find another dead end. We will give you a new way of gaining confidence in bold strategies that change the direction of your business, because you will be able to now know the chances of your strategy succeeding, calibrated against a verifiable yardstick of corporate performance.

In the sports world, golf announcers can tell the odds that a pro will make a putt of a certain length, because the data on all the putts by all the pros have been compiled. Football stats buffs can tell you the odds that a team will win based on the score, the quarter, the number of first downs, and the name of the quarterback, because all that data have been aggregated across league games over many years. The same sort of data is now available about corporate strategy.

Making big moves happen

To get ahead of ourselves a little bit: The data show, in particular, that many companies are simply not bold enough—their strategies are not designed for *big moves*. All too often, the result is incremental improvements that have companies just playing along with the rest of their industries.

We are sure you've seen it yourself: Even if there is a major business opportunity and someone comes in with a breakthrough idea, it tends to get whittled down. The idea feels too risky; too different from what other players are doing. Some people might feel left out. It seems safer to come up with a plan that just varies slightly from last year's, to spread resources across the whole business rather than bet heavily on the break-out of one single unit.

"I used to to be incentivized to underpromise so
I could overdeliver. Now I just hide under my desk."

We recently saw one CEO ask his team for aggressive growth plans. He got them back and liked many of them—only to have to cut back because there was no way to fund them all. In the end, he did not want to frustrate all but a few of his team by disproportionately allocating resources to the likely break-outs, and instead granted some resources to all the businesses. Needless to say, none of them were funded well enough to achieve a real breakthrough. Another CEO asked his team for bold moves and received an M&A idea for growing a new service business in the US. The idea passed a rigorous due diligence process, but then he got cold feet. Yet another CEO came up with a plan to leapfrog to 5G mobile communications technology that would have provided a temporary competitive advantage in Europe, but then felt the board was unlikely to approve that bold plan and self-censored the proposal to protect himself. He settled on a plan that was not much more than an extension of the past.

Our research indicates that to make sustained progress relative to competing businesses, you need to, foremost, choose the right markets to compete in, but also to pull hard enough on at least some of the levers we've identified to clear well-quantified thresholds. The good news is: These big moves do not come at the expense of increased risk. In fact, our data show that the biggest risks might lie in not moving at all.

This might sound a bit fluffy for now, but as you go through the book we will get you the hard data you need and the factual insights to support your decisions.

The journey ahead of us

We intend to take you now on a journey through the strategy room that will eventually get you to a better chance of knowing the right big moves—and to an understanding of the social side of strategy that will let you actually execute those moves. For now, we will leave you with the assertion that our insights dovetail. The data—the outside view—play a big role in giving you a chance to successfully address the problems caused by the social side of strategy and its drag toward inertia, toward small moves that feel safe.

In many ways, our insights resemble the discoveries of behavioral economists, which trace all the way back to Herbert Simon in the 1950s but which have really gathered steam over the past couple of decades with both Daniel Kahneman and more recently Richard Thaler earning Nobel Prizes in Economics. Traditionally, economists considered everyone to be acting rationally, which led to rigorous-seeming curves that were easy to comprehend but in the real world rarely predicted actual behavior. It turned out that people don't view their lives as a series of utility curves. Behavioral economists shed light on how people think and behave.

Like these behavioral economists, we have learned that purely rational approaches—the next 3 × 3 matrix, the latest best-practice case studies—rarely help in achieving breakthroughs in strategy. But observations of what's really going on in the strategy rooms—and in the boardrooms of corporations all over the globe—give us hope that it is actually possible to generate an outside view that will improve the quality of strategy and, consequently, business performance. After a long series of spirited discussions with many of your peers and our partner colleagues around the world, we feel ready to shed new light on what's going on in the strategy room.

Based on our empirical observations and insights, we will take the strategy discussion out of the realm of the theoretical and into the realm of actual behavior, then lay out our data so that you yourself can shape new, more fruitful conversations with your team.

"I DON'T KNOW MUCH ABOUT STRATEGY BUT I KNOW WHAT I LIKE."

If we do this right, you will have a chance to raise your game in many ways, so that you:

- Improve the quality of strategy proposals that are discussed in your strategy room
- Engage in a very different, more collaborative and learning-oriented strategy dialogue with your team
- Experience more authenticity, more rigor, and better challenges in your strategy room
- Make less biased, better strategy decisions, calibrated against the empirics of an outside view
- Lead your team with more courage to make big moves, take calculated risks, and more vigorously commit to the execution of your strategies

To help you tame the social side of strategy, we'll start by exploring why it's so hard to manage. Then we'll lay out a new way of tracking progress based on comparisons against the whole universe of companies, not just against your prior performance or against your industry. We'll go into depth about how to think about the 10 key variables (which we refer to collectively as your endowment, your trends, and your moves), so you can figure your odds of success—and improve them while there's still time. Finally, at the end of the book, we will share with you very practical advice, eight shifts designed to help you change the dynamics in your strategy room. For instance, we will explain how to turn the strategy process from a staccato event into a continually evolving conversation. We'll explain how to get away from spreading resources thinly and actually re-allocating resources to potentially big winners; how to change your focus from setting budget targets and toward generating big moves; how to end sandbagging; and more. These shifts can make your strategy process far more effective and, we hope, a lot more energizing, too.

What will you need to do? Just two things: Get ready to embrace the social side of strategy, and be prepared to throw open the windows of your strategy room to allow for a data-driven, outside view to enter the discussion.

If you are ready to do so, you will experience your own business and your own leadership team in a new way; you will develop better strategies; and you will have a better chance of executing them well. In short, you will have a better shot at beating the odds.

"We're going to exceed last year's performance by doing everything exactly the same."

Chapter 1

Games in the strategy room—and why people play them

Strategy is precisely the wrong problem for human brains and the right problem for playing games, especially when the "inside view" goes unchecked.

Many corporate strategy planning processes begin with a memo like the one on the following page. You've probably seen them before—or written some yourself. They typically lead you and your colleagues to spend months doing lots of work employing sophisticated tools, getting lots of inputs, and using lots of data.

The memo itself is pretty straightforward:

To: Leadership Team

CC: Corporate Staff

Re: Strategy Process 2018

Dear Leadership Team,

With this note, we kick off the strategy cycle of 2018, building on the great work in 2017. We will run the process in three steps:

1. Market analysis due March

2. Key issues due May

3. Full 5-year plan due June

In August, we will discuss the fully integrated plan with the board, from which we will launch the 2019 Annual Operating plan.

We have limited the template to about 50 pages and would hope you have a 10-page Executive Summary in each session so we can focus the conversation on the important topics.

Very much looking forward to our discussions.

S.Miller

Susan Miller, Chief Executive Officer

Templates for our discussions:
["Market Analysis"] ["Key issues"] ["Full 5-year plan"]

After the memo goes out, and after the months of work it kicks off, you generally come up with a solid understanding of what's happening in the marketplace and of the options you have for responding. The CEO leads a series of discussions and formulates a strategy, which the board approves. Then you do the budget . . .

. . . and nothing much happens.

The results are rarely a serious problem. It's not often that you end up having existential issues like those at Kodak, Blockbuster, or Nokia—those high-profile cases get so much attention partly because they're rare. But, even when a strategy "succeeds," the wins too often remain small.[1] The strategy rarely moves the needle very far in the right direction, at least for any length of time. It's not so much that the rocket veers off course in midair; it is more often a failure to launch with enough energy to shoot for the moon. You've spent all that time and effort and only climbed *how* far over the last year?

The social side of strategy, in action

The inside view creates a veritable petri dish that can grow all sorts of dysfunctions once that strategy memo goes out, producing the sort of scenario that we've all seen:

On the Saturday before the strategy discussion, the CEO receives that 150-page document plus appendices as a pre-read. Sigh. The CEO knows that the discussion that's about to start is not so much about the substance. Instead, the process is a sort of management ballet that is choreographed to get a "yes" to the proposed strategy and an approval of the resources requested.

On Monday morning, a presenter starts by giving a market outlook and competitive overview. Someone asks a question about page 5 (we reckon that a presenter has a reasonable chance of making it to page 5 before being interrupted, at which point the serious games around the social side of strategy start). The response might be, "We will cover that on page 42"—knowing, of course, that it's extremely unlikely they'll ever get to page 42 before the end of the meeting (if page 42 even exists). Perhaps the answer is, "We have considered that, and there is an extensive appendix on exactly that question," or, "Good question! Let's take that offline."

We've all seen these little social tricks, right?

Presenters in strategy meetings often seem to not seek a conversation at all. Instead, they appear to deflect as many questions as they can, saying they are "trying to get through the materials." They want to move to the last page of the presentation as smoothly as possible and then get that all-important "yes" to the plan, that "yes" to the resource request, that "yes" to have a shot at the next promotion. A successful meeting is deemed to be one with little friction and maximum good feelings.

Fast forward a bit in the strategy presentation to the discussion of market share performance, or the analysis of strengths and weaknesses. How likely is it for the plan to show low or declining market share? How often does a SWOT[2] analysis come out on the weak side? Those analyses look strong even though we all know for a fact that not every company can win. If one company gains share and gathers strength, others must lose. How often does the presenter arrive at the conclusion that further investments in their own business are not warranted, that the company should consider re-allocating resources to other businesses, cutting back, or even exiting? That just never happens—in strategy presentations, it seems that everyone is a winner. All the time.

CEOs are, of course, no dummies. They have seen these games played before, and many would readily admit that they had to play some of these themselves along the way. Even CEOs would acknowledge giving their plans a risk haircut before presenting them to the board.

Even then, the presenter can still manipulate the data by relying on the inside view. For one, somebody presenting about her business unit has a distinct knowledge advantage over everyone else in the room. Looking at past performance, for instance, should be straightforward, based on 20/20 hindsight—but it's not. So often, there are distortions that are too subtle to catch while conversing in the strategy room. Market share can be defined favorably by excluding geographies or segments where the presenter's business unit is weak. Poor performance can be attributed to one-off items such as the weather, restructuring efforts, new market entrants, or a regulatory change. Markets may be "summarized" in a way that removes all insight—people end up talking to each other about the average temperature of the patients in a hospital.[3]

The dreaded hockey stick

The inside games soon get us to the hockey stick, the icon of the social side of strategy shown in Exhibit 1.

Hockey sticks are everywhere. You might even say that "business plan" is the technical term for a hockey stick. We have all seen the graphs that show revenue and profit heading straight for the sky a few years out: "All that's needed is a bit of an investment for the first year or two, a bit of tolerance for some losses, then you can start booking huge numbers. It's going to be a great business. If we can just get some additional resources today, and you stick with us through a couple of lean years, we'll produce a rocket headed toward the stars."

As many of us have seen from personal experience, these hockey sticks rarely work out, but they are a great way of bargaining for resources for that all-important first-year operating budget. People

Exhibit 1

The Hockey Stick
Does this look familiar to you?

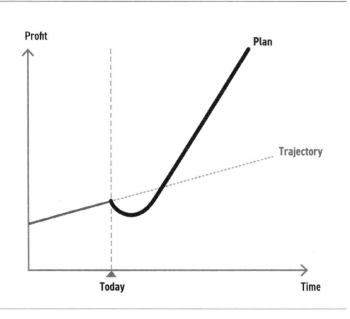

make ambitious claims, arguing that they need a serious amount of resources—all in the full knowledge that they will get negotiated down to half of that. As one CEO told us, "The strategy process is a ritual dance before you get to what really matters: The annual operating plan."

Executives know that failure to have a hockey stick projection pan out generally brings fewer repercussions than not presenting it in the first place. The projections delay the day of reckoning. Who knows? Maybe the plan will work perfectly. Maybe the executive will get lucky, and market conditions will fall just right. Maybe the CEO will forget the grand promise—or maybe a new CEO will be in place by then. Maybe the executive presenting the hockey stick will have moved on. In any case, a hockey stick helps win the argument today, and that's what strategy processes boil down to—the priority is getting to a "yes."

There is one more reason why you can't not present a hockey stick as a manager: Everyone else does it! If you did not do it, even though you know the projection is "off reality," you would send a signal that you lack confidence in your business. Presenting hockey sticks is a ritual, for all to partake in.

So, hockey sticks it is.

Some executives find ways to cut through the gamesmanship. When Jack Welch was CEO of General Electric, for instance, he declared that all his businesses needed to be #1 or #2 in their markets. But, he found over time that business leaders redefined their markets so they could claim to be #1 or #2. He then demanded that everyone come up with a market definition in which they had less than 10 percent market share, thereby creating a breakthrough in the denominator game.[4]

Far more typically, though, the social side of strategy turns the strategy conversation into some form of a beauty contest in which participants want to look good, and the data they present are carefully selected to underscore the right impression. In a speech at the annual global partner meeting of McKinsey, the then-CEO of a major Las Vegas casino operator said: "Whenever I arrive at one of our properties and meet the general manager, he would inevitably tell me that everything is going great—regardless of their actual performance.

They would always deliver an impressive speech on why their business was going well or, if it lost money, why it was just about to get better—a whole lot better. [Sighs] I just wish I met once, just once, a guy who would walk up to me and say: 'Man, things are not well down here, and, to tell you the truth, I can't tell which way is up. I really have no idea why things are heading south—but we are on it, rolling up our sleeves to turn this sucker around.'"

Can we handle the truth?

Why aren't people as open as we wish they were? Why are they politically correct? Remember the movie *Tootsie* and a classic interaction between Michael (Dustin Hoffman) and Julie (Jessica Lange)? Michael has fallen for Julie but has no idea how to approach her. Dressed in drag as Tootsie, and now a confidante for Julie, he hears her lament about how men are always hitting on her and saying she'd love a man who could just be honest. Thinking he's cracked the code, Michael, no longer in drag, says to Julie exactly what she said she hoped to hear from a man. She slaps him. Hard. Then she walks away.

We may think that we want the truth, but, if we are honest, we might not always want it. Jack Nicholson says as Colonel Jessup in *A Few Good Men*: "You want the truth? You can't handle the truth!" We've all learned along the way that bluntness is risky, so we can't even imagine an executive who would tell the CEO that their business unit was in trouble and that they had no idea why. That executive would probably have a lot more to fear than a slap on the wrist.

People's egos, their careers, their bonuses, their status in the organization, the resources they get to fund the growth of their business—all depend to a large extent on how convincingly they present their strategies and the prospects of their business. Think about how far people go in creating "successful" profiles on dating websites—neither the pictures nor the facts have much resemblance to reality, but the goal is to get that first reply and avoid the abyss of being swiped away.

We've all seen these games in business, too. Some managers project vision and competence at the negotiating table, claiming more resources than are warranted. Others sandbag to avoid risky moves and make triple-sure they overachieve on their targets. When everyone else is playing games, why would you stand out as the sole voice of realism?

Playing the inside game

Even though boards and investors are always demanding progress—and we all certainly expect that of ourselves—just holding position is often already an accomplishment. Competition is tough. Think about it: While you're locked up in your own strategy room, the very same discussions are happening across town in your competitor's strategy room, as well. Although we all seem to just focus on the issues in front of us, we are also making the treadmill run a little faster for everyone.

Silicon Valley pioneer Bill Joy said: "No matter who you are, most of the smart people work for someone else."[5] It's true, and competitors will always work diligently to counteract your strategy, or will pursue just about the same opportunities that you see.

But if you're like the vast majority of those in the strategy rooms around the world, you aren't very focused on what's happening in those other strategy rooms or on the smart ideas of your competitors. You're seeing an "inside view" and are playing more of an inside game. The inside view often prevails in strategy rooms because they are tightly sealed. What comes into the room is basically what the participants bring in with them. That is generally a great deal of relevant experience, carried in the brains and memories of a few executives. A lot of data and information comes into the room, too, but it is typically focused on your own company, a handful of key competitors, and your own industry. A lot of information stays outside the room. The air gets stuffy and recycled. People are "reading their own mail."

Strategies can also be constrained because they are being developed "bottom up," as each business unit projects how it will perform over the coming years. Those plans, which are rolled up into the company-wide strategy, are rarely calibrated against outside data to see how similar growth plans historically fared at similar businesses in similar situations.

Nobel laureate Daniel Kahneman explained in his brilliant book, *Thinking, Fast and Slow*, how the realities of the outside world can disappear and be replaced by what he labeled "the inside view." The inside view leads people to extrapolate from their own experiences and data, even when they are attempting something they've never done before. Kahneman says even he has fallen victim to the bias while designing a new syllabus and textbooks for the Ministry of Education in Israel.[6] The team, relying on their experiences in other endeavors, initially projected that they would finish in 1½ to 2½ years. When Kahneman looked at how similar teams had performed on similar projects, he learned that 40 percent of similar teams never finished and that those that did needed 7 to 10 years. The good news is that his team did finish, but it needed 8 years, more than three times as long as they predicted.

The sheer length of the strategy process can also galvanize the inside view. Studies of cognitive biases show that experts become more confident as they gather more data—even though the additional data might not make the experts' projections any more accurate.[7]

Overconfidence is self-reinforcing, too. It leads people to ignore contradictory information, which makes them more confident, which makes them more likely to ignore contradictory information. . . . As weeks and months go by, and the spreadsheets get larger and more detailed, an unwarranted sense of confidence can take hold. It turns out that the more we know, the more dangerous we are. The inside view reigns. We convince ourselves that we have a winning plan this year even though we continue doing pretty much what we've always done.

Look at how precise economic projections are—and how wrong. In the US, the government produces annually 45,000 pieces of economic information, and the private sector generates 4 million more, leading to forecasts that may run to multiple decimal points. The forecasts are reassuring. The prognosticators are smart folks. Yet, most economists didn't predict the three most recent recessions in the US, in 1990, 2001, and 2007, and didn't even see the recessions happening after they'd started. The initial estimate for growth in the US economy in the fourth quarter of 2008 was −3.8 percent. The actual drop turned out to be −9 percent. "Nobody has a clue. It's hugely difficult to forecast the business cycle," said Jan Hatzius, Chief Economist at Goldman Sachs.[8] Yet we still act as though we can predict to a decimal point or two.

Send in the guru

Yes, senior teams sometimes try to complement their inside views by exploring the outside world. One favorite is bringing in a guru. Those discussions tend to be quite interesting and provoke conversation—

surveys at our own global strategy conferences show that people love gurus. We invite them so people find a compelling excuse to come—but how often do their presentations actually influence strategy? You may gain insight into some of the relevant trends, but how are you to act on them? Observing the writing on the wall is certainly easier than acting on it!

Frequently, we are asked to provide information on other industries that faced challenges comparable to the situation at hand. But more often than not, the discussion then ends with the self-reassuring affirmation that "our industry is different," or, "We've been in this industry for 100 years; now this guy comes along and is trying to tell us to do what?" We've had such comments thrown at us regularly—especially before growing a bit of gray hair.[9] The reason? Well, people are often afraid that an analogy or benchmark might suggest that a higher level of performance could be achieved. That means tougher goals, and that might mean lower bonuses. It is not that people do not want to learn. They often like to see the translation of the analogy and performance potential in private meetings—they just do not want to have the discussion in the bigger meeting, not in the strategy room, and certainly not in the boardroom.

The difficulties with today's strategy processes are not news to you? Welcome to the club! More than 70 percent of executives we surveyed[10] say they don't like their strategy process, and 70 percent of board members don't trust the results.

The wrong problem for human brains

Oftentimes, we think that if we can identify a problem then we can overcome it. We're smart people, and our brains and wills are powerful instruments. But there are two reasons that simply knowing about the social problems isn't enough. The first reason is that strategy is done by humans. The second reason is that strategy is done by humans working together.

Let's start with the "done by humans" problem.

While strategy seems as though it should be a purely intellectual exercise, a sort of corporate game of chess, perhaps even played in three dimensions by its best practitioners, strategy problems are exactly the low-frequency, high-uncertainty problems for which the human brain is least adapted.

People are prone to many well-documented unconscious cognitive biases—overconfidence, anchoring, loss aversion, confirmation bias, attribution error, etc.[11] These biases exist to help us filter information for decision making.

Think about one of our ancestors wandering across the plains of Africa. On the occasion of that chap coming across a lion, the chances of him being part of our gene pool today are relatively low if he started to think about the clouds, the beauty of the landscape, or the prospects of finding a meal for the day. They all are possibly interesting or even important topics, but not species-extending in the face of a lion. With fear-induced myopia, our ancestor focused on one thing, and one thing only, and that was getting away when seeing a lion.

So, our brain came with a lot of shortcuts (heuristics, in technical terms) that lurk in the deeper parts of the subconscious mind. They can sure help with day-to-day decision making in our modern lives—we all seem pretty good at that, maybe even extremely good. Just think of how good we are at driving a car; even the dopiest person seems to get by okay on the road. No, the issue is not the daily decisions, where we get countless opportunities to practice and where mistakes yield immediate and possibly painful feedback. Here, our brains have evolved to run on sort of a limbic autopilot like that of the ancestor avoiding the lion.

These unintentional mental shortcuts can distort the outcomes, though, when we are forced to make big, consequential decisions, infrequently, and under high uncertainty. And these are exactly the ones we confront in the strategy room.

Even the most seasoned executives have only limited experience and pattern recognition in these situations. Decisions are taken under uncertainty, and results may not show up for years. In the meantime, any number of human factors, market factors, lag factors, and "noise" can intrude and overwhelm any strategist's ability to predict an outcome. What actually happens may have little to do with the quality of the strategy.

Trying to improve your strategic decision making is like trying to improve your golf game by practicing blindfolded, and not finding out if your ball went into the hole for 3 years.

The biased mind

Consider the decision on whether to donate your organs in the event of an untimely death—it seems a very important one that would typically involve considerable contemplation. But in reality, it turns out that something as minor as the design of the driver's license application form—whether it is an opt-in or an opt-out—makes all the difference. In Denmark, where the program is opt-in, 4 percent of the population donate organs, while neighboring Sweden, where donation is opt-out, reports 86 percent participation. Opt-in Netherlands is at merely 28 percent even after lots of marketing spend, while its opt-out neighbor Belgium reports 98 percent participation. Opt-in Germany is at 12 percent, while opt-out neighbors France, Austria, Hungary, and Poland are all north of 99 percent.[12] The simple explanation is that, when confronted with complex decisions such as signing up for an organ donation program, our minds tend to stall, and we decide—nothing. We tend to go with the form without checking the box, no matter whether it's opt-in or opt-out. The subconscious brain is more powerful than we think.

"HE WAS SHOT BUT LUCKILY THE BULLET HIT HIS ORGAN DONOR CARD."

Here are some of our all-time-favorite biases that we see in strategy rooms:

- **Halo effect.** "Our 6 percent profit growth last year reflected our decision to continue investing in digital, and, in the face of tough trading conditions, we remained ruthless on costs"—a team giving itself a pat on the back even though the whole market also grew profits by 6 percent.[13]
- **Anchoring.** "We forecast 8 percent growth next year, plus or minus 1 percentage point, depending on the demand environment. We will achieve this by pushing even harder on our current projects"—so 8 percent is the starting point of the negotiation, whether or not it should be.
- **Confirmation bias.** "We've put lots of work into analyzing the reasons why this will work" [but no work into the reasons why it won't]. "We've also heard that our top competitor is exploring this opportunity" [so it must be a good idea]. Good luck with trying to stop the momentum for that project.
- **Champion bias.** "We have a great team behind us; we've succeeded on projects like this before. You should have the confidence in us to do it again"—deflecting attention from the merits of the project alone.[14]
- **Loss aversion.** "We don't want to put our baseline at risk by chasing blue sky ideas. We really appreciate the hard work that's gone into alternative strategies and new business lines, but ultimately we think the risks outweigh the benefits"—even though the existing baseline might be under threat.

"Your budget targets would carry more
weight if you told us who you are."

When you bring together a bunch of people with shared experiences and shared goals, they typically wind up telling themselves stories, generally favorable ones—and we are in the perfect den for these biases to flourish. A study found, for instance, that 80 percent of executives believed that their product stood out against the competition—and that 8 percent of customers agreed.[15] This sort of confirmation bias is why people read publications with the same political bent that they have. People may try to challenge themselves, but they really want to nod their heads as their beliefs are confirmed.[16]

Perceptions can also matter more than reality. Respect for past achievements, for instance, can play a big role. A legendary engineer promoted to lead the switching business of a European producer of telecom gear had literally all his resource requests for the old core business approved at will, until the company had completely missed the transition to router-based networks and became an acquisition target.

Strategy processes are also prone to survivor bias.[17] There is no noise coming from the "graveyard of silent failures" because we only see what happened, not what didn't happen.[18] We read all the case studies about great companies that succeeded, with explanations rationalized after the fact for why they did so. There is lots of talk about Warren Buffett, but we hear nothing about the thousands of investors who decided in the same year as Buffett to start buying into businesses, but failed. We can precisely measure the behavior of the customers we have, but what about the silent voices of the customers we don't have? Our experiences are more shaped by learning from survivors, and in a way, we all are "survivors"—our strategy rooms are fraught with biases related to not having failed big-time.

Strategy processes really are in the running for the world's biggest zoo of frolicking biases and social distortions.

Now . . . add social dynamics to the mix

As hard as it might be to overcome those individual biases, they are only part of the reason why you can't just understand the social problems of strategy and assume that you'll then be able to overcome them. Yes, as soon as you introduce people into strategy, you get biases. Then, when you introduce other people—that is, when the approver is different from the doer—you get agency problems.[19]

Don't get us wrong. We have a lot of respect for the people involved in the strategy process. They often are the smartest, most experienced leaders in their businesses. We are not suggesting people are either ill-intended, incapable, or both—quite the opposite, actually. People bring a lot of experience, ideas, and energy to their missions. But with them come biases, too.

Agency problems are fueled by incongruences between management and other stakeholders. Here are just a few of the more prominent ways that managers may act in their own interest, and not purely in that of the enterprise and its stakeholders:

- **"Sandbagging."** "I'm not going to put my neck on the line. I'm only going to agree to a plan that I know for sure I can deliver. My reputation is on the line, and I can't risk being the one division that misses budget." The reality is that individuals will often have a different attitude toward risk than their overall enterprise does.

- **"The short game."** "Someone else will be running this division in 3 years, anyway. I just need to milk performance for the next couple of years, get a good bonus and the next promotion—or maybe get poached by our competitor." The motivations of the executive are not automatically aligned to those of the owners.

- **"My way or your problem."** "I know this business and this industry better than the CEO and better than the board. They'll just have to believe what I tell them. If I say it's too hard, it's too hard. If I don't get the resources I ask for, then there's my excuse for not delivering." The line executive has inside knowledge, and often the CEO and board have little choice but to accept their version of the truth.

- **"I am my numbers."** "I get judged by my numbers, not by how I spend my time. I'm just going to work hard enough to hit my targets, but not a lot more." One's supervisor can't directly observe the quality of effort, and results can be noisy signals— were those poor results a noble failure; were those great results dumb luck?

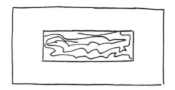

"I don't bother avoiding data and giving in to biases and agency problems. I have people who do that for me."

You have people who you'd hope are all pulling in the same direction, but in reality, they have very different motivations and certainly asymmetric information. While CEOs will try to optimize for the overall success of their companies, those who report to them will for sure care a lot more about their individual business units and about those who work for them. How can they not? We all know that the people whose business thrives will be the ones who get rewarded. People, for the most part, are not bad; they're just perfectly evolved to play the game. In fact, much of a business leader's stature might reflect just how good he or she is at playing it. Based on attribution bias, you are your numbers, so they'd better be good, no matter how you get there.

Let's not forget incentives, either. There are too many to recount all of them here, and they go way beyond financial remuneration. Presenting in front of your superiors or your peers is a matter of pride. Your track record is a matter of ego. Your team wants protection. Charles Munger and Warren Buffett used to say: "95 percent of behavior is driven by personal or collective incentives," only to later correct themselves: "The 95 percent was wrong; it is more like 99 percent."[20]

Strategy involves a complex set of motivations in a complex game. Far from having a single goal that everyone can focus on, executives are negotiating next year's budget, competing for resources, delegating responsibilities to others, maintaining and escalating prior commitments, impressing the board, inspiring confidence among a broader set of stakeholders—all at the same time. They know that they have to craft a strategy that claims to generate a 15 percent increase to get the 10 percent they really want, and they know that the main act is the budget. The strategy discussion is just the opening salvo.

Perhaps the most widely read piece of research that McKinsey has published in the past decade showed that companies that rapidly re-allocate capital to new growth businesses outperform those that take a steady-state approach.[21] Yet, the social side of strategy is such that companies still tend to take what is known as a "peanut butter" approach—spreading a thin layer of resources smoothly across the whole enterprise, even though it's clear that opportunities are far greater in some areas than in others.

With everyone competing so hard for resources, it's tough to make decisions about winners and losers. Picking winners may sometimes be easier, but it's definitely hard to starve a business with less potential, especially if the leader has been around a long time or the business is a big part of the company's history.

No matter the precise motivation, executives will use every bit of social power they have to improve the chances of their business succeeding. We've seen people do all sorts of things. We've even seen one executive, the president of one of the largest consumer electronics companies in the world, be denied the resources he felt he needed and then rally loyal members of the board to get the CEO fired. That story, by the way, did not end well for the insurgent, who was soon ushered out the door, nor for the company. But the point is: Even if we don't like to acknowledge it, we are social creatures and covet status in the tribe. This was an excellent trait from an evolutionary perspective, when it was important to be the big gorilla in the jungle, but can be an obstacle when developing good strategies.

When the inside view remains unchecked

The best breeding conditions for creating a flawed strategy are when the inside view remains unchallenged, creating a false sense of certainty about what will happen. Many—in fact, very many—people do strategy as if they were the only horse in the race, almost ignoring that competitors are making strategies, too. People try to throw good money after bad so past decisions don't reveal themselves to be mistakes. Those in the strategy room are confident because they have accounted for all the risk they can see—not realizing that the perils are in the risks they can't see. So often, good performance is attributed to superior management, and bad performance is blamed on market conditions.

Kodak's failure to adapt to digital photography has become a classic example of strategic failure. The story has been told enough, so we will resist the temptation to recount it entirely, but let's highlight the role of the inside view.

We have personally experienced the early advantage Kodak had in digital photography, after one of its researchers in the mid-1970s invented the sensor that is used in digital cameras and after the company was early to market with a consumer camera in the late 1990s. Yes, the camera looked like a brick, and the pictures were a bit grainy by today's standards, but they were good enough for one of the authors of this book to take it as the only camera on his honeymoon trip to Australia—see the original 1997 picture below (not bad, eh?).

Kodak clearly was in the game early on.[22] But people who were involved in the strategy process at Kodak back then say that the real problem was that management never got past their inside view. Film, chemicals, and paper had been around for so long that management could simply not imagine a world in which people didn't light up at the prospect of collecting their prints in little yellow boxes. Even more daunting was the fact that the traditional film business had been generating gross margins of more than 60 percent for a long time. It was hard to cannibalize a business that had sustained those performance levels for decades—especially because the margins in any consumer electronics business were expected to be much lower.

The assumption that the traditional film business would always be around simply never got sufficiently challenged in the strategy room, even though ample evidence to the contrary was available—including at Kodak, which had done a major study in the early 1980s. Kodak management never seriously debated whether digital might turn out to be a superior technology. They spent half a billion dollars developing a camera, the Advantix, that was fully digital but still used film and generated prints—the digital capabilities just let you scroll through images to decide which ones you wanted to print. The camera bombed. Customers simply didn't love prints as much as Kodak's strategists thought they did.

By now, business magazines and literature have assembled a rather impressive list of similar cases where once-great companies ran into difficulties when trends changed the game, or their business models ran out of steam: Circuit City, Sears, Grundig, and Wang, just to name a few. So, today's strategists are more likely to try to find an outside perspective and to bring it into the strategy room—but the inside game still makes it hard to act. For most businesses, the best predictor of next year's budget is still this year's budget, plus or minus a few percent, of course.

Strategy processes often generate a high-level commitment to making a change, but, too often, as with a failing dieter or cigarette quitter, the processes don't surface and deal with other prior commitments that immunize companies against change. As one CEO told us, "If you want a big idea done, you have to pursue it to the last detail. Just because the group said 'yes' doesn't mean it's going to happen."

Bringing about change in the corporations of today reminds us of an attempt to move an octopus, when one leg of the octopus is totally committed to going to the next rock but the other seven remain completely committed to holding on to the rock they're already grasping.

• • •

Just changing mindsets won't be enough, though. The social side of strategy won't give up the fight that easily. A golf instructor won't help much by telling you: "Don't slice." He must give you something positive that you can actually do to solve the problem. Hence, we'll now lay out the empirical research that will provide you with an outside view.

We'll begin by giving you a new way to map out your competitive situation, then show you where you need to go. It's going to be a bit of a journey, so stick with us.

Chapter 2

Opening the windows of your strategy room

The Power Curve built from the economic profits of thousands of companies gives a fresh "outside view" of the universe of strategy as it really is.

Before Christopher Columbus sailed for the New World in 1492, maps of the world were very detailed—and very wrong. A typical one looked like the Fra Mauro map on the following page.[1]
Mapmakers, who had experience with Europe, drew that continent reasonably accurately—here in the middle right of the chart (you have to turn it upside down because back then south was at the top). That's Spain a fraction inside the black dot at the middle on the right, followed by the southern tips of Italy and then Greece as your eyes move left across the Mediterranean.

But the mapmakers back then also drew Africa and Asia just as confidently, despite little knowledge of those unexplored coast lines. Not surprisingly, they missed the Western Hemisphere entirely. The map didn't make any distinction between the up-close, familiar Mediterranean territories and the myths crowding the farther edges of the map. The map ended up being really full—no space for curiosity left in there. Thus, when Columbus sailed west from Spain, he thought he was some 4,000 miles away from

Japan, when he was actually 12,500 miles away—with an unknown continent in between.

After Columbus hit that new continent, at what we now call the West Indies, mapmakers realized just how much they didn't know and began limiting themselves. They drew only what they knew and left blank spaces for the explorers to fill in. Maps began to look like the following one—the Diogo Ribeiro map from 1529.[2] This had the outline of the East Coast of the new continents there in the middle but left the rest for later, and what's more, was the right way up. In just a generation, the map of the world had been irrevocably transformed—a true paradigm shift.

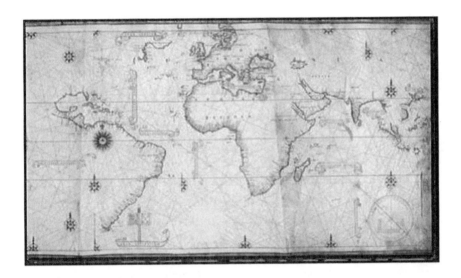

The continents aren't, of course, named North Columbus and South Columbus. They're called North and South America, named after an Italian, Amerigo Vespucci, who played the smallest of roles in the early voyages. He won the honor because, while Columbus and many others never gave up the certainty of those old maps, Vespucci speculated in two texts that the islands that Columbus found were actually part of a new continent. A mapmaker accepted that argument in 1507 and, mistakenly thinking that Vespucci had discovered the continent, named it "America" in his honor. When that map became popular, others adopted the name, and he was immortalized. All because Vespucci was willing to challenge assumptions.

Yuval Noah Harari argues in *Sapiens: A Brief History of Humankind*, that the blank spaces on the new maps didn't just provide the right template for the Age of Exploration, they also ushered in the Scientific Revolution.[3] He believes that the doubts manifested in these "modern" maps guided an entire class of scientists to leave blank spaces for others to fill in, as knowledge increased in many scientific fields. The embracing of ignorance had to come before the embracing of knowledge.

Upon reflection, we thought that the current state of strategy at times reminds us a bit more of those early maps: Good insights from a close-up view, and surrounded by a detailed and compelling narrative with lots of analysis. It might feel as if the strategy room is jammed so full with slides and facts from the "inside view" that there is little leeway for curiosity and wonder about what the external view would say. There is simply not enough room left for uncertainty and exploration. By no means do we want to imply that we discovered a new continent, but we thought it might be helpful to start with conceding that the map for navigating corporate performance is not perfectly understood, yet. With that, we set out to add some information to the map by bringing in an "outside view" to help you chart a new course for your own business toward better performance.

Now we commence our own tour of discovery.

The right yardstick

Let's start creating the new map by setting a clear yardstick for good strategy—a proper compass to guide the way.[4] Some would look at gains in share price, but that struck us as too mercurial, too dependent on the starting and ending dates of the measurement, and maybe also a bit too influenced by factors outside the control of management. Others would look at growth in revenue, yet others at earnings or cash flow. So, could one metric be the yardstick for business performance? Probably not, but *economic profit* comes pretty close, we think.

At its heart, business strategy is all about beating the market, or in other words defying the power of "perfect" markets to push economic surplus back to zero. Economic profit—the total profit after the cost of capital is subtracted—measures the success of that defiance by showing what is left on the table after the forces of competition have played out.[5] Of course, businesses also pursue other objectives, such as delivering inventions, securing employment, or making social contributions and building communities. But if good strategy succeeds in taming market forces, residual economic profit will grow, making it also easier to accomplish the other objectives.

Oddly, you won't find economic profit in many audited financial statements, and our surveys find it is rarely used in the world of strategy. Some executives even asked us, "Didn't we just throw EVA out the window?" Well, we're bringing it back.[6] We believe it is a good metric, as it shows both by how much a company has beaten the market and the scale of that success. Not only does economic profit measure margin and scale, it also incorporates margin development, sales growth, and cash flow.

If we have to choose one variable to measure an enterprise—or at least its purely economic contribution—economic profit could be it.

Because we do lots of presentations on this work, we often get asked: "But what about returns to shareholders, or NPV?" Growth in economic profit drives shareholder returns but is much less noisy and more under control of management. We found that, over a period of 10 years, the top quintile of companies based on growth in economic profit delivered the strongest total shareholder returns (+17 percent per year) while the bottom quintile delivered the weakest (+7 percent per year). Economic profit captures the two parameters we know are driving share price performance over time: return on invested capital (ROIC) and growth.[7] Besides, there are many commercial enterprises that are not listed on public markets, so economic profit is a more universally applicable measure.

Let's get to know this yardstick a bit better (Exhibit 2). From 2010 to 2014, the average company in our database of the world's largest companies reported $920 million in annual operating profit. To make this profit, they used about $9.3 billion of invested capital, including the goodwill spent on past acquisitions.[8] Dividing one by the other gives a return on invested capital of 9.9 percent. But investors and lenders in the average company required a return of 8.0 percent to compensate for use of their funds (measured by weighted average cost of capital), so the first $740 million of profit just made them whole. That left $180 million in economic profit: The spread over the average company's cost of capital multiplied by the scale of its business.

Exhibit 2

The strategic yardstick you can't afford to ignore
We use economic profit as a measure of value creation

Annual average, 2010-14, N=2,393

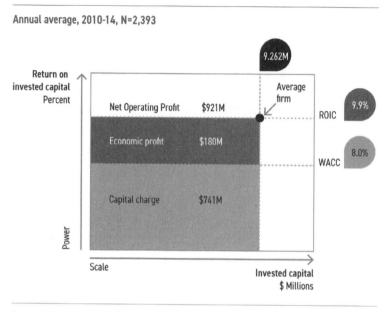

Source: McKinsey Corporate Performance Analytics™

Your business lives on a Power Curve

Once you plot all the economic profits in an ordered line, you find they demonstrate a power law—the tails of the curve rise (and fall) at exponential rates, with long flatlands in the middle.[9] You get this chart, pictured in Exhibit 3, called the Power Curve.

To produce this chart depicting the Power Curve, we took financial performance data for 2,393 of the largest non-financial firms by revenue over the period 2010 to 2014 and estimated each company's average economic profit.[10] The Power Curve shows each individual company's average economic profit over those 5 years ranked from the lowest to the highest. Then we separated the Power Curve into three regions: the bottom of the curve, represented by the bottom quintile of companies; the middle of the curve, represented by the second, third, and fourth quintiles; and the top of the curve, represented by the top

Exhibit 3

The Power Curve of economic profit
The global distribution of economic profit is radically uneven

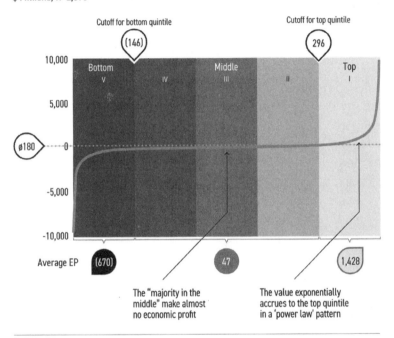

Average annual economic profit generated per firm, 2010–14
$ Millions, N=2,393¹

The "majority in the middle" make almost no economic profit

The value exponentially accrues to the top quintile in a 'power law' pattern

1 Firms with EP above $10b and below -$10b (7 firms) not shown for scaling purposes
Source: McKinsey Corporate Performance Analytics™

quintile of economic profit. There's a big gap from the middle to the top—the average economic profit on the top is 30 times greater! So, if you're not at the high end already, the aspiration of joining the top-tier players should probably be on your mind.

There are many instances of power laws in large data sets from economics, demography, and nature. The distribution of earthquake magnitudes follows such power laws, and so does the distribution of income for pro footballers, or book sales, for that matter. Another example is Zipf's Law, which notes that the most frequent word in English ("the") occurs approximately twice as often as the second-most frequent ("of"), three times as often as the third-most ("and"), and so on. Remarkably, this example of a power law holds for any language.[11]

While we expected a broad distribution of results for economic profit, the steepness of the tails surprised us, as did how flat the broad middle was. Going back to our maps analogy, we thought we were headed for Japan and hit the West Indies instead. And the tails are even steeper if we include the true outliers of economic profit: Companies like Apple live on Mars, two floors up from the profit curve of "ordinary companies." They might inspire mere mortal business leaders— but, practically, they don't fit on the scale of the chart (although they are included in our data set).

Among other things, we realized that the extremes of the results render an average all but meaningless. If Jeff Bezos walks into an ordinary bar, the average wealth of the other people in the room would soar to more than $100 million, even though all the other customers' wallets remain just as slim as before. The "average" footballer's salary doesn't mean much, given the huge spread of figures. This is what life is like on a Power Curve.

What we see on the map

Back in the strategy room, the Power Curve is not the map actually in use. Our inside view gives us a detailed look at how we compare with last year, with our immediate competitors, and with our expectations for the next year. But when we zoom way out and look at the landscape of profitability—at all major companies in all industries and geographies—we get an important new perspective. We see that the vast majority of profits are at one end of the curve and improve exponentially as you get closer to that end. So, good strategy shouldn't focus narrowly on last year or on next year or on competitors. The goal of strategy needs to be to move to the right on the Power Curve. For most businesses, all those in the middle three quintiles, the practical challenge is how to escape the broad, flat middle of the curve and move up into the region on the right, where most profits accrue.

We aren't saying there isn't any value in doing better than last year. Of course there is. Nor are we saying that every company can make it to the top of the Power Curve. Garrison Keillor had his fictional Lake Wobegon, where "all the women are strong, all the men are good looking, and all the children are above average." Just as there is no Lake Wobegon in Minnesota, there is no performance panacea that can enable exceptional performance for all. But zooming way out and looking at the whole landscape of economic profit gives you a very different perspective relative to what you see when you just focus on last year and next year. It gives you a map to explore when charting your strategy.

When we show the Power Curve chart to CEOs, it always leads to a good conversation, driven by curiosity about where they rank. Mostly, the initial reaction is that this is common sense, but not commonly applied. It is not deeply appreciated just how long and flat the middle is, nor how very high the mountains are. There are several important insights we gain from the Power Curve:

Market forces are pretty efficient. Textbook theory says that economic profits should tend toward zero over time, because they get competed away. We're happy to report that, in most industries, profits are possible because real markets aren't perfect. The average company in our sample companies generates returns that exceed the cost of capital by almost 2 percentage points. But the market is chipping away at individual companies' profits all the time. That brutal competition is why it's so hard just to stay in place and why hockey stick plans so seldom turn into reality.

How many times have you seen that $100 million improvement program fail to drop money to the bottom line because all it did was keep your relative cost in line with your competitor? Rather than beating the market, the program was just part of playing along. You were keeping up with the Joneses.

For companies in the middle of the Power Curve, the market is taking a heavy toll. In that flat part of the curve, all the hard work that people in the companies are doing often amounts to not much more than paying the rent. Companies in those three quintiles delivered economic profits averaging just $47 million a year. The discussion about the flatness of the curve in the middle simply isn't taking place in the strategy room now.

The curve is extremely steep at the bookends. Companies in the top quintile capture nearly 90 percent of the economic profit created, averaging $1.4 billion annually. This is a hall of fame for business, with the top 40 companies including household names such as Apple, Microsoft, China Mobile, Samsung Electronics, Exxon, Johnson & Johnson, Oracle, Vodafone, Intel, Cisco, Nestle, Merck, Walmart, Coca-Cola, Audi, Unilever, and Siemens.[12] The full list of top-40 companies earned $283 billion combined annual economic profit, more than half of the combined value for all 2,393 companies in the database ($417 billion).

Overall, the companies in the top quintile average some 30 times as much economic profit as those in the middle three quintiles, while the bottom 20 percent make for deep economic losses. That unevenness exists within the top quintile, too. The top 2 percent together earn about as much as the next 8 percent combined. In smartphones, the top two companies—Apple and Samsung at the time—earned virtually all the economic profit. Yes, all the other mobile phone makers in aggregate destroyed value during that period. Apple earned more "re-selling" memory in its iPhones and iPads than the entire memory industry making those very chips managed to capture.

At the other end of the curve, the undersea canyon of negative economic profit is deep—though, fortunately, not quite as deep as the mountain is high.

The curve is getting steeper over time. Back in 2000–4, companies in the top quintile earned a collective $186 billion in economic profit. Fast forward a decade to 2010–14, and the top quintile captured $684 billion in economic profit. The bottom quintile generated a collective loss of $61 billion in 2000–4. A decade later, the bottom quintile was losing $321 billion. Not surprisingly, investors seek companies that offer market-beating returns. As they do, more capital flows to the top. Managers may be able to fool their bosses, but they can't fool investors. Capital doesn't recognize or respect geographic and industry boundaries. Companies that started in the top quintile 10 years earlier soaked up 50 cents of every dollar of new capital in the decade up to 2014. This capital infusion enabled the top performers to grow their average economic profit by more than 130 percent in real terms over that decade, from $612 million to $1.4 billion, even though their average returns on invested capital stayed relatively constant at around 16 percent.

Even as the curve gets steeper, this is not a permanent inequality. As we will discover during the course of this book, companies and entire industries move up and down the curve. It is uneven but also very dynamic: A firm's place on the curve changes all the time.

Size isn't everything, but it isn't nothing, either. In choosing a measure like economic profit, we know that size comes into play. That might create some feelings of discomfort.[13] One might argue that a relative measure—such as economic profit margin or return on invested capital—should be used. But incorporating size in the measure makes sense: We evaluate the strength of a strategy based not only on how powerful its economic formula is (measured by the spread of its returns over its cost of capital) but also on how scalable that formula is (measured by how much invested capital it could deploy)—see Exhibit 4. Compare Walmart, with a moderate 12 percent return on capital but a

Exhibit 4

Returns vs scale

There are many combinations that can get you into the top quintile

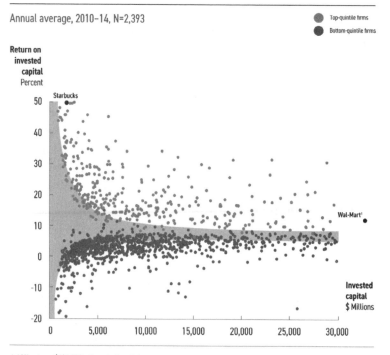

Annual average, 2010–14, N=2,393

● Top-quintile firms
● Bottom-quintile firms

1 12% return, $136,000m invested capital

Source: McKinsey Corporate Performance Analytics™

whopping $136 billion of invested capital, with Starbucks, which has a huge 50 percent return on capital but is limited by being in a much less scalable category, deploying only $2.6 billion of invested capital. Both are top-quintile companies, but which had the better strategy? Well, that's a bit of a moot question as they both generated enormous value, but the difference in economic profit generation is substantial— $5.3 billion from Walmart versus $1.1 billion from Starbucks.

Size has its limitations, too. Larger firms (above-average invested capital) make up 80 percent of all firms in the bottom quintile. If anything, we could say that larger companies are more likely to generate very high or very low economic profit: 28 percent are in the top quintile while just 41 percent of large firms are spread across the middle three quintiles. To say it simply: It is easier to make a big profit or a big loss if you are big. However, it is really the combination of scale and spread that matters.

In the end, it's you versus the world. You're used to comparing against your next-door neighbors and your own last 3 years, but it feels different looking at the whole world as it's represented on the Power Curve. Your horizon gets broadened, and you may be either chastened or emboldened, depending on where you find yourself on the curve— you look at lots of relative data today, but you can now see the whole playing field. This is where companies compete for the eye of the investor in terms of the performance they deliver—relative to all other companies, and not relative to their industries. This is where you see how effective strategy is over time in terms of moving companies up and down that curve. Some feel that it's unfair to be compared against companies in other industries and other nations—but that's the comparison that capital makes. It flows to the best opportunities, no matter the industry or geography. Your main competitor is the Darwinian force of the market that squeezes your profitability; your main measure of whether you are winning is the extent to which you avoid that squeeze.

Why you are where you are

Even CEOs and CFOs are often surprised to see where they are on the Power Curve. It's not that they suffered from delusions; it's just that they're accustomed to an inside view. They compare their performance to peer benchmarks within their immediate competitors, not against the global universe of companies.

Some CEOs are surprised to find themselves in the middle; they feel they are on top of their game or their industry. Some CEOs are surprised to find themselves at the very top of the curve and ponder whether it is their task to expand the curve or their fate to slide down. Wherever a company is, the question quickly becomes: *Why* are we there?

That question, too, leads to a surprise. The tendency when taking an inside view is that, when things are going well, we attribute results to our management's unique recipe; when times are tough, it's an industry problem or bad luck. However, our analysis shows that a good 50 percent of your positioning on the curve is driven by what's happening in your industry—highlighting that "where to play" is really one of the most critical choices in strategy.

Industry performance, we found, also follows a Power Curve, with the same hanging tail and high leading peak, as shown in Exhibit 5.

Exhibit 5

The industry Power Curve

Industries also have a Power Curve—where you play really matters

Average annual economic profit of firms within each industry, 2010–14
$ Millions, N=2,393

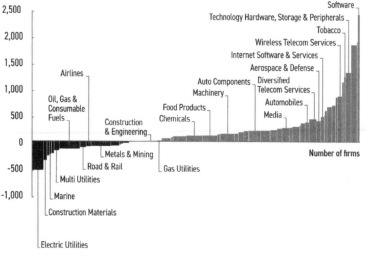

Source: McKinsey Corporate Performance Analytics™

There are 12 tobacco companies in our research, and 9 are in the top quintile. Yet there are 20 paper companies, and none is in the top quintile. Well-known high performers such as software, pharmaceuticals, and wireless telecommunications jostle for position in the top quintile, while utilities, transport, and construction materials lumber along in the bottom quintile.

The role of industry in a company's position on the Power Curve is so substantial that you'd rather be an average company in a great industry than a great company in an average industry—see Exhibit 6. The median pharmaceutical company (India-based Sun Pharmaceuticals, with economic profit of $424 million), the median software company (Adobe Systems, $339 million), and the median semiconductor company (Marvell Technology Group, $277 million) all would be in the top quintile of chemicals companies and the top 10 percent of food products companies.

In some cases, you'd rather be in your supplier's industry than in your own. For example, again in Exhibit 6—the average economic profit of airlines is a loss of $99 million, while suppliers in the aerospace and defense category average a profit of $453 million. In fact, the 20th percentile aerospace and defense supplier, Saab AB, earns more economic profit than the 80th percentile airline, Air New Zealand. That is not to say that all airlines have poor economic performance (witness Japan Airlines), nor that all is rosy in aerospace and defense. But it is a fact of life that there are more and less attractive playing fields.

Across the whole market, firms in the top quintile of the Power Curve get a boost of $335 million of economic profit just from being in better industries, while those in the bottom quintile suffer a penalty of minus $253 million from being in worse industries, as shown in Exhibit 7.

There are, of course, exceptions that don't conform to the fates of their industries. For example, companies from integrated telecommunications services (a top-quintile industry) are over-represented in both the top and bottom company quintiles. The same is true for integrated oil and gas (a bottom-quintile industry). But when it comes to explaining variance we find that industry explains somewhere between 40 and 60 percent, and, as industry definition gets more granular, the share of economic profit explained by the industry effect only increases.

Even though all strategy presentations we've seen start with an industry view, that view is rarely carried forward to explain past performance.

Exhibit 6

Variation in economic profit within industries
Better to be average in a good industry than good in a poor industry

Annual economic profit, 2010–14
$ Millions, N=2,393

● Firm in industry
● Industry mean

Economic profit (log scale) ────────────────────→			# firms	...of which in top quintile
Bottom quintile	Middle quintiles	Top quintile		
Construction Materials			26	4%
Paper & Forest Products			18	0%
Oil, Gas & Consumable Fuels			153	19%
Airlines	Air NZ ○	JAL ○	36	8%
Transportation Infrastructure			11	9%
Chemicals			117	14%
Food Products			109	8%
Media			54	37%
Textiles, Apparel & Luxury Goods			33	39%
Aerospace & Defense	Saab ○		31	42%
Semiconductors & Semiconductor Equipment	Marvell ○		27	48%
Wireless Telecommunication Services			34	53%
Tobacco			13	77%
Technology Hardware, Storage & Peripherals			38	32%
Pharmaceuticals	Sun ○		43	58%
Software	Adobe ○		15	60%

Source: McKinsey Corporate Performance Analytics™

Exhibit 7

The industry effect
Average industry EP boosts the top—and penalizes the bottom

Average annual economic profit, 2010-14
$ Millions, N=2,393

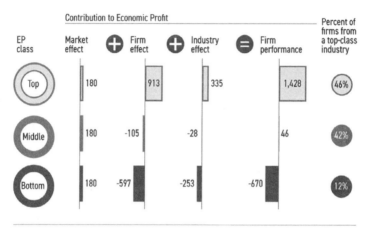

Source: McKinsey Corporate Performance Analytics™

The old wisdom in strategy is that you have to know the real answer to the question: "Why do I make money?" Industry is a much bigger reason than most people understand or want to accept, both on the upside (when tailwinds help us sail along) and on the downside (when the writing on the wall tells us tough times are coming, and we don't like the news).

Now that we have started drawing our new map and understand the crucial role of industry, let's head back to the strategy room and see what's different.

A fresh perspective with the outside view

When you realize that success is very much defined by your company's and your industry's movements on the Power Curve, your perspective changes. Some companies have a low probability of making it to the top quintile, perhaps because of the industry they're in, but many at least have a shot. If you are aspiring to such a move, you are probably contemplating by now a few intriguing insights:

- The **Power Curve is a new reference point** you might not have used before. You're no longer comparing yourself with last year or your neighbor, but rather the full universe of companies competing for capital and economic profits.
- Success for your strategy becomes **moving up on the Power Curve.** Small success is moving in the middle flatlands. Big success is moving to the top quintile, and the reverse holds true for failure.
- Your **aspirations need calibration.** Incremental improvements aren't enough to get you moving, because your competitors are also working hard—and thus all your work might yield just a standstill.
- Moving up on the curve is not a 1-year exercise—it is a **journey that needs good strategy and sustained execution.** The mountain is just too steep at the tails to climb quickly.

The billion-dollar question, of course, is: "What does it take to move on the Power Curve?" Well, almost a billion dollars: As we'll see later, companies that do jump up from the middle quintiles to the top experience an average lift of $640 million in annual economic profit.

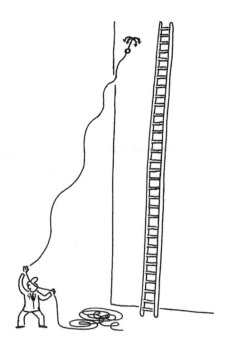

As we've said, success requires bigger moves than companies typically make. One client CEO traditionally framed discussions around 4–6 percent growth and resourced his divisions accordingly. One year, he did a much more granular analysis (business/country) and realized that one geography—Russia at the time—was growing at 30 percent. He swamped the Russian operations with resources, created a much more favorable environment, and it ended up growing much faster. The head of the Russian unit remarked, "I knew we could win; it's just that until now, we never got the resources we needed—all because we used to just look at averages."

Sometimes, big success requires even more drastic measures: Moving into a more profitable industry or more favorable industry segments (tough to do) or, if that's not in the cards, restructuring the economics of your industry to make it more attractive might be your only alternative.

• • •

In setting strategic goals, most companies see hockey stick plans that rarely deliver the results they aspire to. The curious thing is that all of them are actually looking in the right direction. The way to make a move on the Power Curve is, in fact, a hockey stick. The challenge is telling a real one from a fake one. Shortly, we'll get to how you identify real hockey stick plans, but first, let's look at how fake ones are generated, and the problems that result.

Chapter 3

Hockey stick dreams, hairy back realities

Hockey sticks plans are a natural outcome of the strategy game, and are too often coupled only with timid moves. When successive hopeful forecasts pile up against reality, you get the ugliest chart in strategy: the hairy back. But, real hockey sticks do happen!

In a recent survey, CEOs attributed only 50 percent of decisions on target-setting and strategy to facts and analytics—50 percent! The other half they attributed to the strategy process and the dynamics in the strategy room.[1] So, tasks like setting the right ambition levels and priorities are not just difficult technically, they also take place right at the intersection of the biases and agency problems we've discussed.

The tasks are deep in the territory of the social side of strategy, where collective aspirations collide with individual fear, ambitions, rivalry, and bias. Even when the environment is perfectly understood, target setting is noisy. Overconfidence, blind extrapolation, competition for resources, the treadmill of rising expectations, or the typical desire for a goal setter to add "stretch" can cause targets to be set too high. "Sandbagging," negotiations, and risk aversion will cause targets to come out too low.

The consequence: hockey sticks and hairy backs.

The rise of the hairy back

As we've seen, the dynamics in the strategy room often lead to hockey stick plans: overly conservative for the first couple of years, then overly aggressive longer-term.[2] These lines sail upward on the graph after a brief early dip to account for up-front investment. Over the years, unrealized hockey sticks string together, and the ugly cousin of the hockey stick appears, the "hairy back." A real example of one of these—we have a drawer full of them—is shown in Exhibit 8.

Look familiar? (Do try this at home!)

Exhibit 8

Hairy back of reality
A succession of unrealized hockey sticks sprouts a hairy back

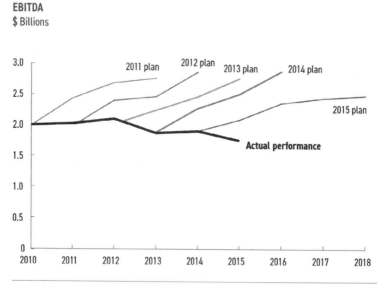

EBITDA
$ Billions

SOURCE: Disguised client example

Exhibit 8 shows the performance of a major multinational. The company planned for a breakout in 2011, only to achieve flat results. Undeterred, the team drew another hockey stick for 2012, then 2013, then 2014, then 2015, even as actual results stayed roughly flat, then trailed off.

Hairy backs are common—in sales, profit, utilization performance, you name it. Boards fear them, investors know them, and CEOs try to avoid them, but they keep happening.

Some stem from overconfidence, a very human trait. When asked about their driving skills, 93 percent of US drivers and 69 percent of Swedish drivers said they were above average. Asked to rate their safety, 88 percent of US drivers and 77 percent of Swedes put themselves in the top half.[3] These biases are shared by experts in many fields—the more experienced people are, the more likely they are to suffer from overconfidence.

Social dynamics in businesses reward overconfidence: Who ever got promoted based on a growth forecast that didn't sail upward? Some, raised on a diet of self-help books, may even believe that setting "stretch goals" will motivate people, no matter how unrealistic these targets may be. So, quite a number of hockey sticks appear because people actually believe they can pull them off.

Getting to yes

Others appear because people are playing social games: While the planning process is officially about strategy, the real goal is to get a "yes" for resources in that all-important budget for next year. Those resources are how managers maintain status and position themselves for the kinds of results that might get them promoted, even perhaps to the top job. Managers don't assume they'll get everything they request; they come in with a big ask so that, even after the expected haircut, they'll get "adequate" resources. Besides, the punishment for not getting resources is generally greater than for not having a hockey stick pan out.

You've seen the game—and probably even played it. When a requirement is set, such as a 15 percent internal rate of return on investments, plans magically morph to just clear that bar. Nobody ever walked into a planning session intending to get a "no" to a plan. Nobody ever wants to lose the competition for resources.

Imagine a manager coming into the room with a realistic but flat target. You'd wonder: Is this person capable or ambitious enough? Has he really thought through his strategy with any creativity or flair? Doesn't he trust his ability to execute? No, hockey stick it is. It's so much easier to believe what we want to be true.

The CEO won't approve every hockey stick but needs a growth story somewhere. Executive teams make lots of decisions, and it's hard to evaluate all the content all the time, so the hockey stick plan that gets backed generally comes from the person with the best track record. The CEO takes a version of that plan to the board, which may push back on some details but generally supports the plans of the CEO.

That's not the end of the story.

A haircut from finance

Then the CFO, doing his or her job to arbitrate resources, gets hold of the plans, and the next phase of the game begins—the one that gets to the ultimate goal: that all-important first-year budget. The CFO, of course, can't live with any performance dip that a hockey stick shows for the first couple of years, the "valley of investment," when results decline before the major growth kicks in. Too much cost-cutting would be required to cover for that dip. The dip would also consume the safety cushion the CFO wants to have in the budget to cover for the downside caused by something unexpectedly going wrong over the course of the year, as it always does. The CEO, while supporting the hockey stick aspirations, also recognizes the need for a cushion—there isn't much worse than missing your numbers after assuring the board you're safe—so the CFO gets to pull back resources, "smoothing out" the first year of the performance curve.

Here is an email in one of our inboxes that typifies the point. Debriefing from a meeting with the global CFO discussing a major strategic re-orientation of a business unit, another executive wrote:

> [She] believes in the strategy but wants—like any good CFO—to see how it can be done without the short term earnings hit. She homed in immediately on the key issue of whether to spend on accelerated capex in the next 2 years.

Regardless of whether a hockey stick was overly optimistic, the result of social gaming, or a real opportunity, this is usually the point when it becomes all but certain that the promised success won't materialize. The investment that was supposed to lay the foundation for growth has taken a haircut—but, for some reason, all too often the ambition level for growth remains largely unchanged.

At the end of the first year, sure enough, performance isn't living up to the hockey stick promise. Attribution bias kicks in. The problem can't be the fault of those cutting the investment. After all, managers signed off on their budgets. The missed target is then blamed on the most convenient cause available, which is usually some one-off event—unseasonable weather, an IT outage, etc.—even though such one-off occurrences seem to happen every year. With failure dismissed as an externality, the management team closes ranks and decides to double down and re-establish the goal. "We lost a year, but we're going to get back on track."

The next hair sprouts.

As Daniel Kahneman and Dan Lovallo explained in their work on the human tendency toward bold forecasts and timid plans, we're inclined to see exceptional growth in sales, earnings, and other metrics but won't make the big moves that could generate those results.[4] They published their paper 25 years ago, but we keep making the same errors. In essence, we are saying: "We're going to do a ton better next year by doing the same things we did this year, or maybe just a little more."

Bold forecasts

Mark Twain beautifully summarized the typical problem with bold forecasts when he said, "It ain't what you don't know that gets you into trouble. It's what you know for sure that just ain't so."

There is a lot of "we know for sure" around. In our speeches, we often ask, for fun, how many people in the room believe that "the Great Wall of China is the only man-made object visible from space."

It continues to blow our minds that most people "know" that to be true—except it isn't.

The claim, first made in 1754, has been known to be untrue since 1961. The first cosmonaut, Yuri Gagarin, checked it out when he orbited the Earth that year. He was unable to pick out the Great Wall with his naked eye, and no space traveler since then has, because the wall is made from rock that is indistinguishable from the surrounding terrain. Yet most people still "know" that the Great Wall is visible from space.

When it comes to forecasting, several silent killers can creep into our strategy room. Some of the most popular ones include: a lack of a proper baseline, errors about performance attribution, and, especially, the ways we deal with uncertainty.

The lack of a proper baseline. Our forecasts are built on things we believe we know. During the first Internet boom, one of our clients was considering investing $1 billion in a new fiber-optic cable network across the US, based on the estimates of explosive growth in communication. It was clear that the advent of the Internet would fuel demand for fiber capacity, and many rushed in to stake a claim. The more the Internet revolutionized business and how people transacted, the more fiber capacity would be required—everybody "knew" that. But that explosive, seemingly unlimited demand wasn't the whole picture. There was already a lot of fiber in use, and its capacity would increase at the rapid pace at which the routers that dispatched signals through the fiber improved. Then there was "dark fiber" to consider (installed capacity that was yet to be used), plus the announced plans of competitors for installing additional capacity. Add it all up, and the expected capacity would exceed even the most outrageous demand projections for the following 5 years. Because the company took the time to do a proper baseline and saw that what everybody "knew" just did not translate into a need for additional capacity, the company decided to stop the project and saved itself the $1 billion allocated to that hockey stick. The fact that barely a year later the Internet bubble imploded was merely icing on the cake for their decision. Many others had invested without a proper baseline, simply acting on what they thought they knew—and paid dearly for it.

Another evergreen problem with baselines is planning for market-share gains. In the early days of the personal computer, every electronics company worth its silicon decided it could capture 20 percent of the rapidly expanding US market, ignoring how many others were staking that same claim. Eight companies tried for 20 percent—the industry hopelessly overbuilt, and the shakeout was painful.[5]

Bold forecasts are hard to avoid. It's too easy to pull cells across the screen in Excel without paying heed to how hard it might have been to just get to the current point. You, like us, might have friends who plan to hit great times in a marathon but fail to meet their expectations because they undertrained, firmly believing that they were already much fitter than they actually were. Businesses make the same sorts of mistakes.

Errors in performance attribution. Errors in assessing business momentum are also easy to make. Often, performance is mistaken for capability: "We've done well, so we must be better than our competition and will continue to prosper no matter what"—even though external conditions may have contributed to the success. These types of momentum mistakes are harder to spot when you're doing well, because the need to understand the underlying dynamics feels less urgent. If a company is prospering in an environment where it can raise prices rapidly, for instance, it may convince itself that it is becoming ever more efficient in its sales operations—simply because the costs of sales are outpaced by revenue growth. When the pricing environment stiffens, however, the company may discover all kinds of inefficiencies that crept into the system.

During the dot-com boom, several North American consumer electronics contract manufacturing companies expanded rapidly by acquiring factories of their customers left and right. Their share prices rose exponentially around stories of unmatched efficiency and logistics capabilities. When the growth story ended with the bust of the Internet bubble, it came to light that, during the rapid growth, even the most basic integration of newly acquired operations had been neglected, exacerbating the effects of dropping volumes. The recovery took years, and several companies became acquisition targets themselves.

We are prone to attribution errors even when they hurt us. We all cherish, for instance, the "friendly" family doctor. However, patients of doctors who are in the top quartile for customer satisfaction are associated with 9 percent higher medical costs and 25 percent higher mortality rates. A doctor who makes you feel good can put you in danger[6]—but try telling that to a happy patient.

A realistic perspective on corporate performance also tends to get obfuscated by stretch goals—or BHAGs (big hairy audacious goals). In setting those, leaders often put hope over facts. Managers with exceptional track records seem especially prone to willing their way to performance by setting unrealistically high performance bars—at times with negative effects on the morale of their teams.

Many business books help to extend the perception that greatness can be easily achieved. Building from selected case studies, they imply that there is exceptional performance waiting just around the corner—as long as you adopt the right formula. It ain't. For a start, this loose causality ignores the gigantic role of industry dynamics. Not everybody can be an Apple, no matter how long we cite them as a heroic example. In fact, probably nobody can (more precisely, in our sample, 1 out of 2,393 can). Still, books are written, and people try, secretly attributing more capabilities to themselves than they have.

How we deal with uncertainty. "Predictions are difficult, especially about the future," quipped Yogi Berra and, before him, Niels Bohr.[7] This rings especially true when trying to run a proper strategy process. Uncertainty is not only everywhere in and around strategy, it is the very reason why we need strategy. Without uncertainty, we'd just need a plan to go from A to B.

The problem in dealing with uncertainty in the strategy process is not so much the analysis. While uncertainty is often missing from the analysis—and even proper scenario planning is still rather rare—the issue is, surprise, the social side of strategy. Why? At some level, it is easy for the CEO to deal with uncertainty by playing a portfolio game, knowing that not every bet has to pay off for the total play to work. The problem is that what is a portfolio game on the corporate level becomes a matter of all-in commitment for an individual business unit leader. We have all heard the saying: "You are your numbers." The saying isn't: "Well, that project only had a 50 percent chance of success, so I won't hold failure against him until he's had another similar failure or two." No, at the level of the unit leader, results are pretty much binary. You make it, or you don't.

It's the very existence of probabilities and uncertainties that allows the social game space to flourish.

The issue is noisy signals. We can't really tell if that poor result was a noble failure, inasmuch as we can't tell if the great result was blind luck. Was it a case of best efforts on a good bet but a bad roll of the dice? Was it a more pernicious failure of planning or execution? Was it, perhaps, just a bad strategy to start with? Uncertainty doesn't only mean we can't see around the *next* corner; uncertainty also invades the past. That dust cloud in the rearview mirror means you can't really tell where you came from.[8]

Of course, in running a business, there are many elements that you just can't control—the fate of the economy, political events, and your competitors' actions. In most strategy rooms, the question on how to deal with uncertainty looms large. It's the 600-pound gorilla in the room. Actually, it's sitting in the middle of the table, it has long teeth, and it's drooling. Nobody wants to talk about it—it's a complex topic that can easily get in the way of getting a "yes" to the plan. But it's sitting there. So, managers presenting strategies have sophisticated approaches on how to deal with the gorilla. They have to get to a "yes," not a "maybe." That means they have to inspire confidence in the outcomes they are promising—providing at least an illusion of certainty.

Here are some of our all-time favorites among the ways that people deal with uncertainty in the strategy room.

First, **ignoring uncertainty.** Many strategy presentations we see start with an analyst-based projection of the market. Not scenarios, not a range of outcomes: They start with a "most likely version of the future." And that's the last thing you heard about uncertainty in the presentation. From then on, you get single-point estimates for the plan, too, and it's a straight shot for the "yes."

What about treating **uncertainty as an afterthought?** The strategy room is a harsh place for most, and, quite frankly, failure on that stage is not an option for most managers. Execution problems? Okay. A strategy that has gaps? We can fix that. But a strategy conversation about probabilities? You must be kidding! The result is a slide about risks on page 149 of a 150-page strategy deck. The presenter hopes to win a "yes" on funding before getting anywhere close to that far into the deck. That slide on page 149, titled something like "Potential Risks and How to Mitigate Them," is there just so the presenter can say the issue is covered if the odd question about risks should pop up.

Finally, **pretending to deal with uncertainty.** In some cases, uncertainty is actually discussed in the strategy room. Say, geopolitical risks are threatening sales growth in an emerging market, or a competitor could make an industry-consolidating move. There will be a few scenarios, plus a discussion on which of them would be more likely or less likely to emerge. Then, one scenario is picked as "base case," and that's probably the last thing you hear about uncertainty. Strategy clear, job done.

There are, of course, businesses that could not survive without dealing with uncertainty. For example, in asset management and other financial businesses, risk-weighted metrics are normal. The difference is that they are moving money around. In more tangible businesses, you move people and money around—and also the careers and reputations of business leaders. While the calculator loses reputation by wrongly calculating risk, the manager loses reputation by giving up resources.

All these common practices and related errors can lay the foundation for setting the wrong ambition levels and, consequently, flawed strategies.

To be clear: There is nothing wrong about having bold targets. In fact, you need bold targets to move upward on the Power Curve. But those ambitions need to be anchored in the realities of a business and the evolving context it operates in. This book is about how to set bold targets, but to do so in a way that is equally matched by the boldness of the moves needed to achieve them.

Timid plans

A recent McKinsey study of a large sample of big companies showed that over 90 percent of budgets on a business unit level are statistically explained by the previous years' budget levels.[9] Most companies evolve in incremental steps as a result of cautious plans. But how do timid plans gel with overly ambitious forecasts and targets?

Well, it starts with us being human. When it comes to making real decisions, in particular when these decisions have implications for our own families, careers, or wealth, many of us tend to be risk averse.

"HE'S VERY RISK AVERSE."

You might have participated in surveys your bank is obliged to conduct to determine your investor profile. The results of these surveys and many experiments by behavioral scientists clearly show that most of us are much more willing to forgo a large upside to avoid a small downside. We simply do not like losing.

But when that individual risk aversion gets projected onto corporate strategy, we hit problems. A large, diversified corporation with many investors, themselves diversified, will have a far greater risk tolerance than the middle manager who is the gatekeeper to the plans.

The avoidance of downside at almost all costs happens all too often in the strategy room. Big moves are rarely proposed, and even less frequently accepted. The CEO of one of the largest Hong Kong property companies complained to us that none of his managers ever comes up with big ideas. When we asked him why, he responded: "Well, whenever they speak up, they cannot really articulate themselves, so I shut them down after half a minute." Guess what those who spoke up will do in the next meeting?

Think about it: How often have you seen a business unit manager come into the annual planning cycle with a strong M&A strategy? How often have you seen moves proposed that would truly change the game in an industry? That just does not happen that often. Most discussions in the strategy room are about intensifying efforts to gain a few percent more market share or to squeeze out a few more percentage points of margin. That will show progress. Nobody will get fired.

As we've said, we will show that this belief in incremental progress is a fallacy: Bigger moves not only increase your odds of success but reduce the risk of sliding down. Still, the fear of downside risk pervades the planning environment. Nearly 8 out of 10 executives surveyed by our firm tell us that their companies are more geared toward confirming existing hypotheses in their strategy processes than testing new ones. Going for incremental moves is the norm, not the exception.

Corporate peanut butter

Avoiding conflicts in the team, being "practical" about the business, giving every team member a "fair chance," keeping the motivation up—all these arguments contribute to resource stickiness. Corporate planning becomes more like your breakfast strategy: Spreading resources thinly, like peanut butter on bread, across all parts of the business, making sure everyone is covered.

Almost by default, peanut buttering ensures that, even if a hockey stick were possible, it would be hard for a business unit leader to get all the resources needed to pull it off. One of our high-tech clients with a core computing business with $26 billion in revenue wanted to build another pillar for growth. The company even went so far as to free up some resources from R&D and the capital budget. But then it decided to pursue 17 growth opportunities in parallel. When an M&A opportunity came along in an attractive services business, which would likely have provided that growth pillar, the resources to execute the deal were not available because 16 other managers were drawing on them for their respective initiatives. The deal didn't happen.

Corporate peanut butter almost guarantees that you won't make a big enough move to get to the top of the Power Curve.

Shooting for the known

At the other end of the business calendar, when it gets to incentives, bonuses, and promotions, there lies another cause for timid plans. We all want to succeed—of course. But that means that most of us will vastly prefer a P90 plan (one that we will hit with a 90 percent chance) over a P50 plan (which we would hit only 50 percent of the times we try). In fact, a lot of people we work with would quietly admit they only agree to budget targets that they feel confident they can hit almost for sure (P100), save any completely unexpected disruptions. Yet, when we ask CEOs what would be fair, in terms of misses, many of them say that every 3–4 years a leader should miss a plan if the plan has been stretched enough; i.e., P60 to P75 plans. What a difference in perspective!

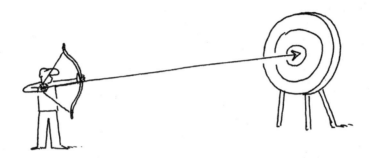

The head of operations for a large high-tech industrial company (actually, the same one we just mentioned) told us recently: "We were beaten up badly earlier this year for missing a target. I'm not going to risk that again—I understand we might get to gold standard performance by the end of the year, but let's first get to the performance level written in the annual plan and then see where we go from there." The problem being that, by that time, any chance of reaching the more ambitious target by the end of the year had passed.

With all the timidity baked into us and into the process, even bold plans can't shake the lethargy.

Here's the really confounding thing, though: While hockey sticks routinely produce the dreaded hairy backs, real hockey sticks do exist. And those real hockey sticks are how companies typically make major moves upward on the Power Curve.

Look at the Power Curve: Companies in the top quintile earn 30 times as much as the average company in the middle quintiles. Moving to that top quintile is almost by definition a hockey stick plan that creates enormous value for stakeholders. They do happen, but how?

"Occasionally in the strategy room we'll see
things as they really are and where they're
going and come up with a truly bold plan.
Your job will be to talk us out of it."

Real hockey sticks

Take a look at Exhibit 9. The gray line is the typical company—one that starts in the middle quintiles and is still there a decade later. The black line started in the same exact place but was one of the companies to make it to the top quintile over the 10-year period. That black line sure looks like a hockey stick—a dip for the first 4 years followed by rapid progress.

Satya Nadella is CEO of Microsoft because he produced a real hockey stick. When he was promoted in 2011 to run a business at Microsoft that included its cloud services, the cloud was a small part of his business, which in turn was a modest-sized part of the whole company. But Nadella saw so much potential that he devoted almost all his personal time to the cloud business, along with an outsized proportion of his total resources. The business grew rapidly from revenue

Exhibit 9

Real hockey sticks

Firms that jump up the Power Curve produce real hockey sticks

Average economic profit
$ Millions relative to year 2000, for 1,435 firms starting in the middle 3 quintiles

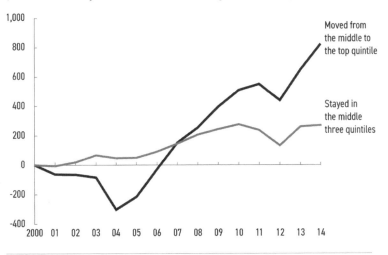

Source: McKinsey Corporate Performance Analytics™

in the hundreds of millions to several billions, and Nadella was named CEO in early 2014.

When NXP, the former semiconductor division of Philips, was spun out to private equity in 2006, the top team aggressively re-allocated investments, given the winner-takes-all nature of the industry. NXP divested large and prestigious areas, such as chips for mobile and digital that consumed huge resources, and made big bets on chips for identification and automotive uses. The hockey stick growth of the chosen markets led to a five-fold increase in market value over the following decade.

• • •

Real hockey sticks do exist. The issue is separating the few real ones from the many fakes. The conundrum we are facing is that we should doubt every hockey stick—yet we often need one, if we're to move up the Power Curve.

So, what does it take to actually move on the curve?

Chapter 4

What are the odds?

Strategy plays out in a world of probabilities, not certainties. But the odds are knowable: Eight percent of middle-tier companies manage to jump up into the top quintile of the Power Curve over a decade. But which ones?

Once you've recognized the perils of the social side of strategy, you need a new paradigm. Consider poker and golf. In general, the more that skill is involved in a game, like golf, the less you need to think about probabilities. If we played a world-class golfer, say the likes of Bernhard Langer or Rory McIlroy, we could be quite sure that we'd never win in a match against them, probably not even on a single hole. The more that luck (uncertainty) is involved in a game, like poker, the more you need to ponder the odds. In poker, we'd not only have a chance to win a hand against a world-class player, like

Phil Hellmuth with his record 14 World Series of Poker bracelets, but would even occasionally beat him in a tournament, as people actually do. Hellmuth would certainly beat us *over time*—and we are probably well advised not to play him—but, in the short run, we'd have a chance.

Don't get us wrong. Business is obviously a matter of skill, of great skill. You don't just have cards dealt to you. You work hard for the assets and talent that you get to deploy. But there is uncertainty, and strategy is about how to deal with it.

In any game, as in business, your goal needs to be to give yourself the best possible odds, and to think in those terms. People shouldn't just get credit for winning and demerits for losing. If five companies each have an 80 percent chance of succeeding, that still means that one will usually fail. If five companies each have a 20 percent chance of success, one of the five is still likely to win. If all we see from these 10 companies together is five wins and five fails, it would be wrong to look at all of them the same way. Clearly the superior strategy is the one with an 80 percent chance of success, and this is the one that should be given the credit, no matter whether you win or lose.

Risk, of course, needs to be part of the probability discussion, too. If you have just a slim chance of winning, but a bet costs you little and the potential win is huge, that still may be an investment worth making. The converse is true, too. An expensive investment that generates a high probability of a small success may be a bad idea. Poker players refer to the calculations as "pot odds." If a $100 bet gives you a 20 percent chance of winning a $200 pot, you fold. Essentially, you're paying $100 for $40—that 20 percent of the $200. But a $100 bet that gives you a 20 percent chance of winning a $2,000 pot is one you make every time, because you're paying $100 to get $400—20 percent of $2,000. So, an assessment of your odds—competitive, market, regulatory, etc.—needs to be part of your calculation.

"Forget the odds of success. I want the odds we'll keep our jobs if we mess up."

Leicester City's soccer team showed us in the 2015–16 English Premier League season that anything is possible, no matter the odds. The team, in earlier years sometimes relegated to the third division of the English Premier League, had made an improbable run through the second division and into the first division but was considered to be such a long shot for the 2015–16 championship that bookmakers said there was a greater chance that Elvis Presley was still alive than that Leicester City would win the Premier League . . . and then Leicester City won the title.[1]

As much fun as that was—many called it the biggest upset in the history of sports—we don't like to bank on being the exception. We always should assume we're going to be the rule.

Okay: What are the odds?

The knowable probability of success

We ran the numbers and can report that, at the highest level, your odds look like those in Exhibit 10. This chart shows the odds of making a move across the quintiles of the Power Curve over a 10-year period, if you started in the middle three quintiles.

Exhibit 10

What are the odds?
There is an 8 percent chance of jumping from the middle to the top

Percent of firms
N = 1,435 firms starting in the middle 3 quintiles

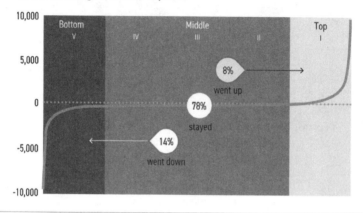

Source: McKinsey Corporate Performance Analytics™

Your odds of going from the middle quintiles of the curve to the top quintile over a 10-year period are 8 percent.

8 percent!

Let that sink in for a moment. Fewer than 1-in-10 companies make such a gain over a 10-year period. In the strategy room 10 years ago, you can imagine how many companies actually planned for such a performance improvement. Some might even have been convinced that they could pull it off. Probably most had their plans approved.

Not even 1 in 10 made it. Wow. Those are tough odds.

Another way to show this is in Exhibit 11. The matrix tells you, based on where you started, what the odds are for where you'll end up. You should start getting familiar with that number 8 on the diagram—it's on the end of the middle row, which tells you the odds of ending in the top if you started in the middle.

Exhibit 11

The mobility matrix
The odds of where you end up depend on where you start

Percent likelihood, N=2,393

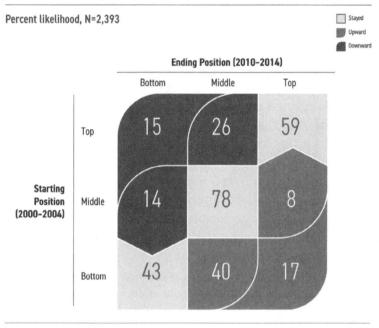

Legend:
- ☐ Stayed
- ▨ Upward
- ◤ Downward

Ending Position (2010-2014)

	Bottom	Middle	Top
Top	15	26	59
Middle	14	78	8
Bottom	43	40	17

Starting Position (2000-2004)

Source: McKinsey Corporate Performance Analytics™

Next, look at the light gray diagonal reading 43–78–59, which tells you the odds of ending in the same location where you started. Turns out, the entire curve is rather sticky; it is hard to achieve any mobility at all. 78 percent of firms in the flat middle stayed put, and pity those 43 percent of bottom quintile firms that were still stuck there 10 years later.

Now look at the top row: those firms that started at the top. They have a 59 percent chance of still being in that quintile 10 years later. Nice. But that means you have a 41 percent chance of moving down the Power Curve, including a 15 percent chance of ending up in the bottom quintile.[2]

Now, plenty of firms are just going to move within the middle tier. The efforts to continuously sustain and upgrade performance are very important, and companies can deliver great results for shareholders by steadily improving their position on the curve. It's just that—given the extreme non-linearity of the curve—the giant leaps matter exponentially more.

The odds of individual business units moving up and down the curve are roughly the same as for companies. And, when companies make a big move up the curve, it is mostly because one, or at most two, of their businesses make a hockey stick improvement. When we looked at 101 companies that moved up at least one quintile *and* for which we had business unit–level data, in two-thirds of the cases it was just one of the units that moved up.

Think about that for a moment. If you have a portfolio of 10 businesses, chances are that only one will make a hockey stick move over a 10-year period—and correctly identifying that one and feeding it all the resources it needs will most likely determine whether the company as a whole can make a significant move up the Power Curve. This insight about the need to find the "1 in 10" has huge implications for how you run a multi-business company.

Having a plan that gives you a chance of moving up the Power Curve means, first and foremost, that you choose the right businesses in your portfolio to back. Their chances are 1 in 10 to show real improvement, and you probably only have to pick 1 or 2 businesses correctly.

Flight paths of the upwardly mobile

Just as companies deliver economic profit in very different combinations—remember the discussion we had about Starbucks and Wal-mart?—movements on the Power Curve also result from different "flight paths," i.e., combinations of ROIC and growth performance over time.

When there are big movements up and down the Power Curve, these flight paths are spectacular. Starting from sea level (an average starting economic profit of $11 million a year in 2000–4 for the mid-tier companies), a move to the top generates an extra economic profit of $628 million annually on average, and a whopping

8.9 percentage points in ROIC. That's a gain of almost one point a year.

Descents are just as crushing as ascents are exhilarating: Companies that went down lost $421 million from their annual economic profit on average and compressed their ROIC by 4.5 percentage points.

"HE WAS ALWAYS MORE OF A SHAKER THAN A MOVER."

Some flight paths are more likely to get you to the stars than others. Exhibit 12 shows what happens depending on your performance against the median firm.

- If you underperform on both growth and ROIC improvement, you have virtually no chance of getting off the ground. In fact, you have a 27 percent chance of falling from the middle to the bottom quintile.
- High growth with below-median ROIC improvement gives you a small chance of an upside, but doesn't do much to reduce the downside risk.
- A performance-only strategy that focuses on improving ROIC but does not deliver above-median growth is certainly "playing it safe." You have almost zero chance of going down, but that strategy just gives you sample-average odds of going up to the top quintile, at 8 percent.

Exhibit 12

Odds vs performance profiles
ROIC and growth are best in combination

Odds for firms in the middle 3 quintiles, N=1,435

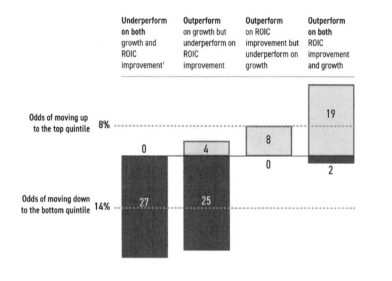

	Underperform on both growth and ROIC improvement[1]	Outperform on growth but underperform on ROIC improvement	Outperform on ROIC improvement but underperform on growth	Outperform on both ROIC improvement and growth
Odds of moving up to the top quintile 8%	0	4	8	19
			0	2
Odds of moving down to the bottom quintile 14%	27	25		

1 *Relative to sample median*

Source: McKinsey Corporate Performance Analytics™

- The magic happens when both growth and ROIC improvements work in concert. Outperforming on both these levers is rewarded by a much higher chance of upward mobility: 19 percent. It is this *increasing returns to scale* dynamic that seems to matter, where each increment of growth makes the business not only bigger but also better. Assets built around common, sharable intellectual property, those with network or platform effects, and those with higher fixed costs enabling massive economics of scale tend to have increasing returns to scale.

What do those data mean for you? Well, if your hockey stick plan does not commit to improvements in both growth and ROIC, you might want to give it some more thought. Getting into the top quintile is harder than you might have expected, and the flight paths to the top underscore this challenge.

A tale of three companies

A look at three companies will help us illustrate the different flight paths that companies can take—as shown in Exhibit 13.

Exhibit 13

A tale of 3 companies
PCC, DNP, and Unfi started in a similar spot but ended in very different places

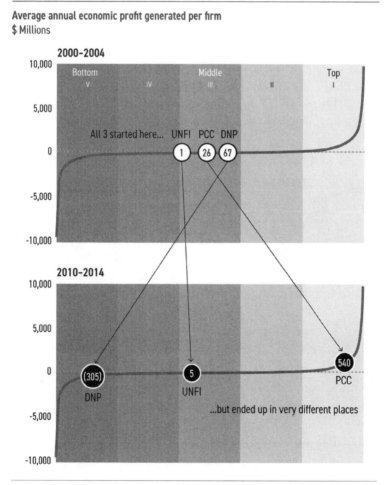

Average annual economic profit generated per firm
$ Millions

PCC is a US-based maker of precision aircraft components (incidentally, owned by Warren Buffett's Berkshire Hathaway for the last few years). Unfi is an American distributor of natural, organic, and specialty foods and related products. DNP is a leading Japanese newspaper publisher.

We picked these three because they started the period 2000–4 as next-door neighbors right in the middle of the Power Curve. Their outcomes could not have been more different, with PCC sailing up, Unfi staying fixed, and DNP sliding down.

PCC pulled off a real hockey stick and went straight to the top quintile, generating a 27 percent CAGR (compound annual growth rate) in total shareholder return. They did this by making four big moves to double down in an industry with a strong tailwind—aerospace and defense. Unfi stayed in the middle of the curve, focusing on making productivity gains to offset the impact of adverse industry trends. DNP dropped to the bottom quintile because it chose to invest heavily, via both capex and M&A, in an industry with strong headwinds—remember that printing was starting to be affected by digital media during that period.

There are many angles to why all of that happened, and we will revisit some of them later, but we can be close to certain that in 2001, in each of their strategy rooms, their leaders were plotting for a move to the top. They were approving hockey stick plans.

They were in good company. Across the Power Curve, everybody is under performance pressure, everybody has high hopes, and everybody is working incredibly hard for a better future. But, as in the case of PCC, Unfi, and DNP, not everybody will see their dreams come true—more important, not everybody has the same chance of getting there. In fact, quite the opposite is true.

Take a look at Exhibit 14. We are admittedly jumping ahead a bit, but take our word for the moment. Imagine you had a model that converted measurable attributes about a company into adjusted (or conditional) odds about how likely they were to succeed. Well, we do! Even though the average is 8 percent, it turns out that the chances of companies in the middle of making it to the top quintile are not only different—they are vastly different, based on our model outputs. Just as the fates of our three companies were very different, so, too, were their starting odds—and they played out those odds.

Exhibit 14

Wide range of odds
They could have known

Percent chance of moving up from the middle to the top, according to our model
N = 1,435 firms starting in the middle 3 quintiles, rank-ordered

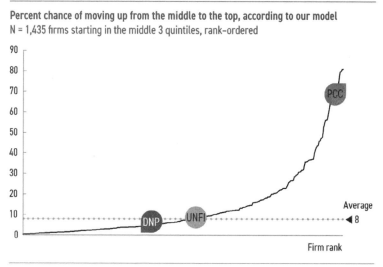

Source: McKinsey Corporate Performance Analytics™

This is intriguing, isn't it? While the odds, on average, are just 8 percent, the odds for individual companies range from nearly 0 percent all the way to more than 80 percent.

If the chances of making it to the top turn out to be so different for each of the companies on the Power Curve, then the question for CEOs, managers, and investors, of course, is: Can those odds only be calculated after the fact, or could they have been known beforehand?

We will explore this question for much of the rest of the book—and what business leaders can do about changing these odds, but let's start with a simple question: Why are the odds of success not in the strategy room when plans are being discussed?

Where are the odds in the strategy room?

Conversations in the strategy room tend to be like those at a consumer goods client of ours, with $18 billion in revenue and the aspiration of achieving double-digit growth. The company did a great deal of planning, and the aspiration looked reasonable. But the company's actual odds of success hadn't yet made it into the room. The plan was built based on an inside view, building from the bottom-up estimates of the business units.

A straightforward bit of research made the company reconsider. Publicly available information showed that among industry peers within the same revenue range as our client, only 10 percent generated sustained double-digit growth over 10 years.[3] The question became: Is our strategy actually better than 90 percent of our peers? Really? What makes us stand out, even though we'd performed like an average company over the prior 5 years, growing in the mid-single digits?

To tell you the truth, bringing the actual odds into the strategy room did not make us very popular with the management team, but they did recalibrate the conversation in important ways. An executive told us: "We had no idea that our value-creation plans were so concentrated on so few areas."

" WANT TO BET NO ONE DARES MENTION THE ODDS?"

While the statistics of moving on the Power Curve are straightforward enough, those odds are rarely discussed in the strategy room. Companies in the top quintile tend to think that's where they belong.

After all, they worked hard to get there and have developed impressive advantages over the competition. Why wouldn't they stay at the top of the heap? Likewise, companies in the middle quintiles tend to believe that they can move up. A chance that they'll drop to the bottom quintile—why bother to even consider that possibility?

We collectively have seen hundreds of strategic plans and can observe that the frequency of a plan for a company at the top of the curve to show a slide down is much lower than the real statistics we assembled for this book. Some plans do suggest a slide down, but not nearly the ~40 percent we observe in the real life of companies.

With odds comes the explicit realization of risks, and loss aversion kicks in. Directly confronting risks can make people gun-shy, even when we're actually interested in having them take more risks. That can be a problem.

The push for certainty

In strategy rooms, there often seems to be a push toward certainty—not odds. The work usually begins by entertaining lots of ideas, and then testing them to winnow them down. Once there are some clear hypotheses, they are tested and refined, with the idea of reducing uncertainty. While we don't always succeed, as those hairy backs show, we certainly attempt to do so. Forcing us to think in terms of probabilities works against that desire for certainty, that consensus that lets us all leave the room united on the plan and ready to execute.

As one CEO in Italy told us: "I can't handle multiple realities." Pushed to consider various possible future scenarios, he said: "I'd rather pick the world I live in." It's much easier to tell people, "You do this. You do that" than to live in a world of probabilistic uncertainty. With probabilities in the room, KPIs become harder to specify.

Spreadsheets aren't exactly built for odds and ranges, either. They're built for specific numbers, so it's hard to start dealing with a 75 percent chance that a value will be between X and Y—multiplied by the thousands of cells in a corporate budget. US President Harry

Truman famously said he wanted a one-handed economist so he would no longer have to listen to his experts say, "on the one hand this, on the other hand that."

You might have heard similar sentiments in your strategy room as people tried to bring discussions to a close. "Life is not a scenario. Make up your mind." "Go left or right, but make a decision." "Probabilities? I don't care what you do in your office, but when you come up here and present, tell us what you think."

Issues of favoritism kick in, too, that don't fit well with odds. As soon as we decide not to "peanut butter" resources and, instead, back business units that have the best prospects, then we're not only picking winners, we're also picking losers. But nobody likes to lose. We all know how hard people will then fight to protect their resources, and we are all prone to protect people who are our friends, or loyal, or both.

" . . . The third little pig wanted to build a wolf-proof brick house. But the other two pigs thought that would take away resources from their budgets, so they talked him out of it right before the wolf killed all three of them."

Bringing probabilities in can make evaluating performance uncomfortably complex. The situation resembles the FBI office that hears about a gang that intends to rob one of three banks. The head of the office dispatches teams to all three banks to catch the thieves. Obviously, only one team will capture the gang, but the entire unit should receive the praise and rewards. But we know that, most of the time, the ones who are in the right place at the right time will be lauded as heroes and rewarded.

You are your numbers

Bill Parcells, an American football coach, illustrated this well by saying: "We are what our record says we are."[4] In other words: Quit claiming moral victories, whining about injuries, and reassuring fans that we'll get better.

Even if you get your management team to think in terms of probabilities, those probabilities might be forgotten at the end of the year when it comes to performance evaluations. Either you made your numbers, or you didn't.

Ed Catmull at Pixar was very deliberate about how to allow for noble failures. He labeled some projects as being "experimental," not aimed at theatrical release, to encourage people to try riskier ideas. He also funded some ideas considered to be "unlikely," so failure did not become a stigma. But he still acknowledges that "We have to try extra hard to make it safe to fail."[5]

If you are going to use odds, you also have to be able to calibrate them precisely—a hard task. Heads of business units will want to get to a "P90 plan"—one where they have a 90 percent chance of succeeding—while having the CEO see the plan as P50. The result is often an unspoken compromise: Stretch targets are set, but with baseline budgets, and the first level of incentive pay kicks in if the baseline goals are met. In other words, the CEO gets her stretch goals, but the executive team also gets softer goals that they expect to meet almost all the time. The problem is that the company might end up not pushing initiatives with the right level of ambition, and consequently not resourcing them appropriately to make a meaningful move up the Power Curve.

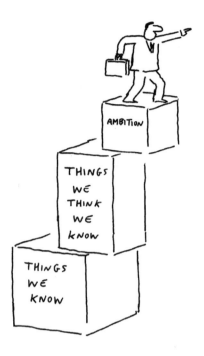

The CEO needs to know what the odds really are, to be able to calibrate goals and compensation appropriately. It's not only hard to set the right goals at the start of the year but difficult to sort out causality at the end of the year, because of the dust that gets kicked up behind you, making the road traveled hard to see in the rearview mirror. Did success come because of managerial decisions and great execution, or because of an error by a competitor and a favorable market? Did problems occur because bad weather killed demand during the key buying season or because managers misjudged their customers? We know how the managers would vote on both questions . . .

A prominent example of where a board got it right was when they appointed Wendell Weeks to be the CEO of Corning Glass in 2005. The board did so, even though Weeks led the company's optical fiber business, which in the dot-com crash of 2001 had taken Corning almost to the brink. That problem was accurately attributed to the worsening market conditions, not management performance. In subsequent years, Weeks became one of the most highly regarded corporate leaders in America, leading Corning to be number one globally in LCD glass and—with the help of "gorilla technology"—number one in smartphone cover glass, as well.

Judge from your own experience, but it strikes us that the clear judgment of Corning's board might be more the exception than the rule in terms of boards and CEOs accurately attributing performance.

• • •

So, where are we now?

We have now given you, for the first time, a glimpse at the probabilities of strategy—the odds that a company will move up or down on the Power Curve—and the notion that the probabilities for individual companies vastly diverge. We've also seen that dealing with probabilities is a challenge for business leaders, but that not properly dealing with them is one of the reason that social games are being played.

Now that the "average" probabilities of moving on the Power Curve have entered the room, the obvious next questions are: What is your own company's probability of success, and what actions can you take to improve that probability? How do you change your odds of beating the market?

We tell clients that a plan that has a realistic chance of producing a real hockey stick that will carry a company from the middle to the top of the Power Curve should have an element of magic to it, something that stands out. Jokingly, we say: "You should be able to smell the specialness through a video conference" if you want to have some confidence that a hockey stick plan is the real deal. In the next chapter, we'll start to go into detail about how to find one.

"I KNOW WHAT WE NEED TO DO BUT I CAN'T BRING MYSELF TO UNCROSS MY LEGS."

Chapter 5

How to find the real hockey stick

You can shift the odds of strategy by capitalizing on your endowment, riding the right trends, and most important, making a few big moves.

For decades, there has been no shortage of advice on how to develop a successful strategy. Yet we still appear to be wrestling with the same issues: How do we tell good strategy from bad? How do we bring the team along? How do we get significant strategic moves executed? One of our former managing directors wrote a paper[1] about inertia and the lack of agility in organizations to execute resource re-allocations . . . in 1973! Why is it that we still are wrestling with the very same conundrums?

What's different this time?

Almost all strategy books that fill your shelves today suffer from a lack of testable hypotheses. How are we supposed to learn whether a recommendation works if the only supporting evidence is anecdotal or based on case examples? There just isn't any way to quantify and test those ideas, which is why lists of great companies fall apart so quickly.[2]

If you look at the three books that sit on more managers' bookshelves than any others—*In Search of Excellence* (1982), *Built to Last* (1994), and *Good to Great* (2001)—they use a common method for learning lessons about strategy. They collect companies that are "great," "excellent," or "enduring" and attempt to infer the formula behind that greatness, excellence, and endurance. The assumption is that, by mimicking the companies' practices, you will be able to mimic their performance.[3] These are certainly good books—more than 10 million readers can't be wrong—and all the companies highlighted in them were truly incredible. However, look at how the 50 companies mentioned performed over the following decades. If you constructed a portfolio of the stocks on the dates of publication and held them, you would have outperformed the market index by 1.7 percent. Not bad at all. *Good to Great* is in the lead at 2.6 percent, followed by *Built to Last* at 1.6 percent, and *In Search of Excellence* at 1.5 percent. But the odds that one of these 50 exemplars outperformed the market were just 52 percent, hardly better than a coin toss, and the chances of a major underperformance were much greater than for a major outperformance—just eight companies beat the index by more than 5 percent, while a total of 16 trailed the index by more than 5 percent.

The prescriptions in these books made sense, but they were somewhat vague—or too specific to an individual company—and it's hard to sort out the winning ideas from the less important ones. *Good to Great*, for instance, says it's crucial for the CEO to be a Level 5 leader. One of the criteria for being a Level 5 leader is that the leader pick a successor who is also a Level 5 leader. Jack Welch, long regarded as one of the best, made an excellent choice when he named Jeff Immelt to succeed him as CEO at GE in 2000. Unfortunately, GE had essentially become a finance company under Welch, which left it highly vulnerable in the global financial crisis of 2008. Although Immelt restructured GE and divested risk-prone parts of the business, GE shares underperformed the market during Immelt's 16-year tenure. A truly recognized Level 5 leader picked another truly recognized Level 5 leader—but the company still underperformed. Circumstances—in this case a financial crisis—can overwhelm even world-class Level 5 leadership.

"Here's where we decided to ignore
all inconvenient data."

Many ideas about strategy provide a lens for looking at history and understanding why something failed or succeeded, but what really matters is having a way of peering into the future, not the past. Knowing the number for yesterday's lottery winner doesn't help so much.

Check the facts

That's why we emphasize the use of deep, testable data. We have examined many hypotheses based on publicly available data about thousands of companies around the globe. This helped identify those corporate performance levers that really matter. We back-tested the data and were able to verify that our model generates surprisingly accurate predictions about the chances of a strategy leading to success. We have deployed the analysis in our work over the past 4 years with clients across the globe and found that it does, indeed, lead to better strategy conversations.

Unlike the data that go into the standard inside view, our research provides reference data on broad characteristics, draws from large samples, focuses on probability, and is calibrated from the top down, so it provides a bulwark against social distortions.

We've explained how the empirics gave us average odds, but now we're moving to estimating company-specific odds based on the company's attributes. The result is a way to calibrate your strategy in a probabilistic world—a score sheet or benchmark for strategies. Equipped with the knowledge of what attributes are most important, we can now predict the quality of a company strategy in advance.

Of course, the social side of strategy won't go down without a fight, but keeping score in a different way can help you shift the conversation.

The odds that matter: Yours

So far, we've talked about the probability of success as an 8 percent chance of moving from the middle to the top of the Power Curve. But unless you're the theoretical average company, the 8 percent is not very helpful for you. Instead, you'd rather know the odds of *your* company and your strategy moving up the Power Curve. Well, we can do this by adding color to the picture, in just the same way that Thomas Bayes helped us understand conditional probability:[4] The more we know about a company, the more precisely we can estimate its odds of success.

Here is a simple analogy: If the only thing we know is that a person is a person, then the best estimate for his or her income is the global average, or about $15,000 per year. If we now add information, say that the person is American, our estimate jumps to the average American income per person, or $56,000. If we add the information that he is an American male, 55 years old, the estimate jumps to $64,500. If that guy works in the IT industry, it jumps to $86,000, and if we know the person is Bill Gates, well, it's a lot more than that.

The same thing needs to be true in our assessment of the probabilities of corporate success. To unpack this idea, let's consider the same companies from the last chapter that all started at the same point on the Power Curve. Based on the average odds, they all had an 8 percent chance of moving to the top quintile. However, their actual destinies could not have been more different. Could they have known this? Actually, yes, they could have.

When we modeled these companies, we discovered that Dai Nippon Printing (DNP) had a 69 percent chance of going down to the bottom quintile, and down it went. Unfi had an 87 percent chance of staying in the middle, and that's what happened. The model scored Precision Castparts as having a 76 percent chance of rising to the top, and the company did get there, indeed.

Odds aren't destiny, of course. If four companies have a 76 percent chance of moving to the Promised Land, that still means that one of them, on average, won't make it and will be disappointed. There's not much to be done about that. But a 76 percent chance is very different from an 8 percent average and should give way to more confidence in support of a strategy. Many companies give themselves only a slim chance of progress, and they're much better off knowing that before they head too far down a dead end. It's also important, if you're the 76-percenter who failed to win the bet, to know that you did the right thing and to be undeterred from making that kind of strong wager again.

Even if you know your overall odds, you need to understand which of your attributes and actions are the most important in determining your chances for success. That knowledge will guide your decisions about where to dedicate your efforts to give your company the best chance of moving up the Power Curve.

"I know that moving up the Power Curve will be tough. But keep in mind that I've survived 30 years of commuting on public transportation."

The highly entertaining article "How to make a hit film" in *The Economist*[5] beautifully illustrates how it's not only possible to know the odds of success, but how it's possible to know what levers to pull to improve those odds (See Exhibit 15):

In 1983 William Goldman, a screenwriter, coined the famous saying that in Hollywood, "Nobody knows anything" when it comes to predicting which films will succeed at the box office.

Exhibit 15

How to make a hit film
Superheroes, super box office

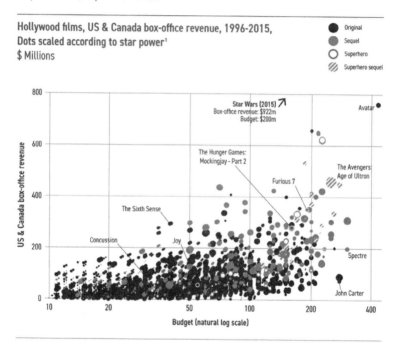

Hollywood films, US & Canada box-office revenue, 1996-2015,
Dots scaled according to star power[1]
$ Millions

- Original
- Sequel
- Superhero
- Superhero sequel

1 Box-office revenue from leading actors' non-sequel films over previous five years

Source: The Numbers; The Economist

To find out how true that remains, we have analyzed the performance of more than 2,000 films with a budget of more than $10 million, released in America and Canada since 1995, to see which factors help make a movie a hit . . .

Our analysis suggests a formula that maximizes the chances of packing them in. First, create a child-friendly superhero film with plenty of action and scope for turning it into a franchise. Set your budget at an impressive but not reckless $85 million. Convince a major studio to distribute it on wide release in the summer (when releases earn an average of $15 million *more than at other times). Lastly, cast two lead actors with a solid but unspectacular box-office history, who are thus not too expensive. With reasonable reviews from critics and the audience alike, your film would make about $125 million at the American box office. But do it for the money, not the plaudits: Such a film would have just a one-in-500 chance of carrying off an Oscar for Best Picture.*

Moving from the box office back into your own strategy room: What similar set of attributes leads to a good strategy?

The 10 variables that make the difference

In our work on the corporate performance data of 2,393 of the largest companies, covering 15 years, 127 industry sectors, and 62 countries, we found 10 levers that are the strongest determinants of your odds of success. We looked at 40 variables and found that 10 of them were key; when we back-tested our model against the 2,393 companies for which we had enough information to place them on the Power Curve, we were 86 percent accurate in predicting companies' movement on the curve over the course of a decade, in terms of whether they would end up in the top, middle, or bottom parts of the Power Curve.

You probably won't be terribly surprised by any of these 10 performance levers—they're all already somewhere on your list of topics. What hasn't been clear until now—after we completed our empirical work—is the importance of these levers, and the degree to which you need to act on them to make a real difference. Our research also shows that some things don't matter as much as you might think for generating a move up the Power Curve. Discarded variables included the amount of *past* revenue growth, and increases or decreases in industry or geographic diversification.

This is, as we've promised, not another framework, but we've decided to group these 10 levers for ease of use into three categories: *endowment, trends,* and *moves.* Once you get your arms around these, you will be able to understand much better your real chances of success—ahead of time, when you can still do something about your strategy and its execution. Your endowment is what you start with. Trends are the winds that you are sailing which are pushing you along, hitting you in the face, or buffeting you from the side. Moves are what you do. Endowments, trends, and moves are like the primary colors of strategy. Now, we just have to mix them appropriately.

We will detail the 10 variables that determine your chances for success. But first let us explain how they work, because the rest of the book will then be much easier. First, they are all measured relative to other companies in the sample—it's not how smart you are, but how much smarter you are than the other kids taking the test. If they did all their homework, you need to have done that and more. Second, to get a boost, you have to cross an upper threshold, and we will show you where these thresholds are. It is binary—much like the Power Curve itself. Getting one point better doesn't seem to do much; you need to put yourself in another league. Same goes on the downside—yes, having a bad score can drag you down, too, but only if you go below a lower threshold. Okay, now we can start the tour.

Endowment

When companies think about their starting point, they often think in terms of their P&L or their market share, but the three variables that matter most in determining your endowment are: your starting revenue (size), your debt level (leverage), and your past investment in R&D (innovation).

1. **Size of your company.** The larger your company is, the more likely you are to be able to improve your position on the Power Curve. That may seem to be unfair to smaller companies or to contradict the success stories we read about start-ups, but when it comes to scaling the Power Curve, size amplifies the effects of performance improvement in absolute terms. Our research found that to have a significant advantage on this variable you need to be in the top quintile in total revenue. Today, that means roughly exceeding $7.5 billion in revenue. No harm if you are not at that level, yet. It's just that you won't get an advantage from scale in terms of your chance of moving up on the Power Curve for now. To illustrate how fast that bar is moving, 10 years ago, $3.3 billion in revenue was big enough to get you into the top quintile for size.

2. **Debt level.** There is an inverse relationship between how much leverage you have built into your current balance sheet and your chances of moving up the Power Curve. The less debt you have, the better your chances of moving up. Your debt capacity indicates how much headroom you have available to invest in your growth opportunities. The key here is to have a debt-to-equity ratio that is favorable enough to put you in the top 40 percent in your own industry.

3. **Past investment in R&D.** This indicates what prospects you've invested in and what you may have to invest in. You needed to be in the top half of your industry in your ratio of R&D to sales, to benefit from a significant improvement in the chances of moving up the Power Curve. For many questioning their R&D organizations about the return on their investments, it might be a source of comfort to see that R&D investments can pay off.

Trends

The two key variables that fall under trends are industry trend and exposure to growth geographies. If your industry is moving up the Industry Power Curve, you're likely to move along with that tailwind. If you're operating in growth geographies, you'll benefit, too, though being in the right countries doesn't matter quite as much as being in an industry that trends upward.

1. **Industry trend.** The trend in your industry is the single most important of all 10 attributes. For your industry to be your friend, it needs to be moving up the Industry Power Curve by at least 1 quintile over a 10-year period. The metric we used is average growth in economic profit across all companies in the industry. This is like the tide going in—or out—and lifting or lowering the average level of boats in the harbor.

2. **Geographic trend.** The key here is to be in markets that are among the top 40 percent for nominal GDP growth. For companies operating in more than one geographic market—most companies among the 2,393 in the database do—you calculate your corporate-wide GDP growth figure based on the percentage of revenue you received from each geographic market. It's intuitively clear that

being exposed to faster-growing markets yields benefits (but equally interesting how overall macroeconomic conditions are a footnote in many long-term strategy discussions).

Moves

Many plans, based on hockey sticks, call for revenue growth equal to GDP and for, say, an increase in margin of two percentage points. That sort of approach could, in fact, let you jump from the middle quintiles of the Power Curve to the top in 10 years. But, remember, only a small percentage of hockey stick projections actually happen. Other companies pursue similar strategies, and the market competes away the improvements through lower prices or more service. Customers benefit—but you just wind up with a hairy back.

Our research found five moves that, pursued persistently, can get you to where you want to go—they work best in combination, but we'll get into that later. For now, here are the five moves we found that matter:

1. **Programmatic M&A.** This one surprises people because they have the idea that studies show that most M&A deals fail (factually wrong) and resist (rightly) the idea of a bet-the-company deal. A key indicator of success is "programmatic M&A," a steady stream of deals, each costing no more than 30 percent of your market cap but adding up over 10 years to at least 30 percent of your market cap.

2. **Dynamic allocation of resources.** Our research found that companies are more likely to succeed when they re-allocate capital expenditures at a healthy clip—feeding the units that could break out and produce a major move up the Power Curve, while starving those that are unlikely to surge. The threshold here is re-allocating at least 50 percent of capital expenditure among business units over a decade.

3. **Strong capital expenditure.** You meet the bar on this lever if you are in the top 20 percent in your industry in your ratio of capital spending to sales. That typically means spending 1.7 times the industry median. That is a big number.

4. **Strength of productivity program.** Everybody is trying to reduce their costs—cutting overhead and improving labor productivity. The question is whether you are improving productivity consistently faster than your competitors. Our research found that the bar is at an improvement rate that's at least in the top 30 percent of your industry.

5. **Improvements in differentiation.** To make business model innovation and pricing advantages improve your chances of moving up the Power Curve, you need to make it into the top 30 percent in your industry in terms of gross margin. This measure captures whether a company has been able to either develop a sustainable cost advantage or charge premium prices because of product differentiation and innovation.

It all matters

Exhibit 16 summarizes these 10 levers—for companies starting in the middle quintiles (the variables are the same, but the values are a little different if you start in the bottom or the top). One way of seeing the relative importance of the levers is to look at how the odds of upward movement change in different threshold regions for each variable. For example, if your company catches an industry mega-trend (your industry moves up at least one quintile on the Industry Power Curve over 10 years), then your company's chances of moving from the middle to the top are 24 percent. Alas, only the best-positioned 20 percent of companies get to enjoy that much tailwind. But if you have a strong

Exhibit 16

The impact of the 10 variables

Your scores will pull you up or down from the 8% base rate of mobility

Percent chance of moving up
N = 1,435 firms starting in the middle 3 quintiles, rank-ordered

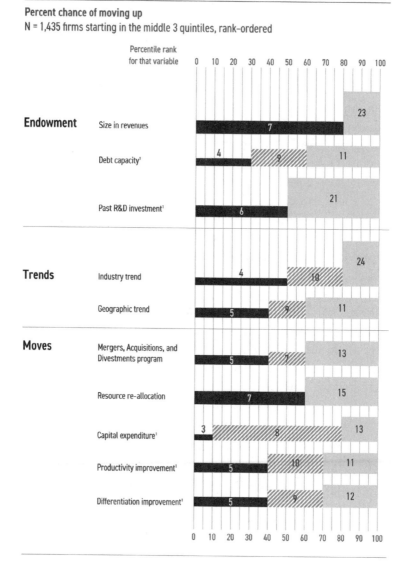

1 Normalized by industry median

Source: McKinsey Corporate Performance Analytics™

headwind, like 50 percent of companies in the sample, the chances of upward movement are just 4 percent. The other 30 percent of companies with a moderate industry trend had a 10 percent chance of moving up. And we compare all these to the overall odds of 8 percent for all middle-tier companies.

If all that seems too complex or boring, the punchline is: The more you can be on the right-hand side of the distribution for the 10 variables, the better your odds. And, the more you are on the left-hand side, the worse your odds. The model we developed for this book is a little more complex than that—because of different weightings and interactions between variables—but not that much more complex. Are you above the threshold, boosting your odds, or below the threshold, lowering them?

Don't be discouraged. In our sample, 60 percent of companies in the middle three quintiles reached our threshold on only two or fewer of the 10 levers.

> **NOTE:** The impact of these levers on your probability of moving on the Power Curve depends on your starting point. If your company is at the top (or the bottom) of the Power Curve, these statistics look very different—and the approach to strategy needs to be tailored. Please refer to the Appendix for a detailed description.

The mobility dashboard

Here is what a "mobility dashboard" looks like for PCC, the company from Chapter 4 that leapt up the Power Curve (Exhibit 17). The circles show which percentile PCC was in for each of the 10 variables. The colors on the bars indicate at what point the score on a single lever starts to change the chances of a company moving up or down the Power Curve—where the thresholds are. If a company scores in the upper shaded zone, the chances of moving up improve. If a company scores in the lower shaded zone of a lever, then there is an odds penalty.

As you can see, in 2004, the endowment scores were unimpressive for PCC, a 60-year-old manufacturer of complex metal components and products for the aerospace, power, and industrial markets.

Exhibit 17

PCC's mobility dashboard
A high score on 5 variables gave PCC high odds of moving up

Increases the odds of upward mobility
Reduces the odds of upward mobility
Percentile score for the attribute

		Percentile 0 — 50 — 100
Endowment	Size in revenue	
	Debt capacity[1]	
	Past R&D investment[1]	
Trends	Industry trend	
	Geographic trend	
Moves	M&A&D program	
	Resource re-allocation	
	Capital expenditure[1]	
	Productivity improvement[1]	
	Differentiation improvement[1]	

PCC's odds of mobility

1 — Down to Bottom
23 — Stay in Middle
76 — Up to Top

1 Relative to industry

Source: McKinsey Corporate Performance Analytics™

Revenue and debt levels were in the middle of the pack, and the company had not invested heavily in R&D. In terms of trends, the geographic exposure was unimpressive. However, the aerospace industry experienced enormous tailwinds over those 10 years, which helped a lot.

Most important, though, PCC made big moves that collectively shifted its odds of reaching the top quintile to 76 percent. The company did so by surpassing the high-performance thresholds on four of the five moves. For mergers, acquisitions, and divestments, PCC combined a high value and volume of deals over the decade through a deliberate and regular program of transactions in the aerospace and power markets. This was a steady diet of transactions, not one-off binges. The last

2 years of our study were typical of PCC's actions through the decade. In 2013, PCC acquired Permaswage SAS—a manufacturer of aerospace fluid fittings—for $600 million and divested its Primus Composites business. This was followed by the acquisition of Aerospace Dynamics—an operator of high-speed machining centers—for $625 million in 2014, or roughly 2 percent of PCC's market capitalization.

In other moves, PCC re-allocated 61 percent of its capital spending among its three major divisions, while managing the rare double feat of both productivity and margin moves, the only aerospace and defense company in our sample to do so. While nearly doubling its labor productivity, PCC managed to reduce its overhead ratio by three percentage points. It lifted its gross profit-to-sales ratio from 27 to 35 percent.

The combination of a positive industry trend and successful execution of multiple moves makes PCC a showcase of a "high odds" strategy and perhaps highlights why Berkshire Hathaway agreed in 2015 to buy PCC for $37.2 billion. And, as Exhibit 18 shows, the rewards for shareholders were obvious.

Exhibit 18

A real-life hockey stick
Four of the five big moves took PCC straight to the top quintile

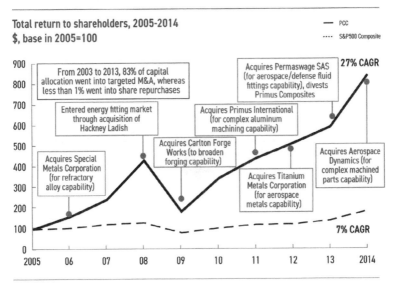

Source: Thomson Reuters Eikon

By contrast, if you remember the other two companies we discussed, Dai Nippon Printing and United Natural Foods (Unfi), both faced industry and geographic headwinds and were not able to do enough to overcome them (Exhibit 19). DNP began with a reasonable endowment but only successfully made two of the five possible moves, so our model predicted a 69 percent likelihood of it sliding to the bottom quintile. And so it did. Unfi only cleared the threshold on one attribute but improved productivity enough in an industry where productivity matters a great deal that our model gave it high odds of staying in the middle ranks. That's also exactly what happened.

Exhibit 19

The better the mobility dashboard, the better the odds
PCC clearly had the better dashboard

Mobility dashboards, 2000–04 to 2010–14

- ● Above the upper threshold
- ○ Between thresholds
- ● Below the lower threshold
- — Not applicable

		DNP	UNFI	PCC
Endowment	Size in revenue	●	○	○
	Debt capacity	○	○	○
	Past R&D investment	—	—	●
Trends	Industry trend	●	●	●
	Geographic trend	●	●	●
Moves	M&A&D program	●	○	●
	Resource re-allocation	○	○	●
	Capital expenditure	●	○	○
	Productivity improvement	○	●	●
	Differentiation improvement	●	●	●
Modelled most likely scenario		69	87	76
		chance of going down	chance of staying put	chance of going up

1 Relative to industry

2 Average percentile ranking against scoring factor

Source: McKinsey Strategy Practice and Corporate Performance Analytics™

To be clear, PCC has been a great performer over that 10-year period, but we are not touting PCC as a great case example. There is no predictive power in this analysis for PCC's performance looking forward beyond 2015. We are simply explaining its success over the previous 10 years and use the example to demonstrate that this success would have been predictable, had we known their strategy and the aerospace industry trend in 2001–4.

Know the odds

In analyzing the odds of moving on the Power Curve across 2,393 of the largest companies in the world, we found that endowment determines about 30 percent, trends determine about 25 percent, and your moves determine about 45 percent of the probability of moving on the curve. While the industry trend is the single most important lever among the 10, it is strategic moves that, in aggregate, explain almost half of the mobility of companies on the Power Curve.

Electrical equipment maker ABB and chemicals giant BASF are examples of companies with strong endowments that leveraged those advantages to move from the middle quintile on the Power Curve to the top quintile over the decade that our research covered. In terms of trends, Japanese automaker Isuzu was helped by strong industry and geographic tailwinds to move all the way from the bottom quintile of the Power Curve to the top. In terms of moves, we've seen how PCC pulled four of the five levers and moved to the top.

While we've treated each lever separately, in reality these attributes work in concert. The odds aren't calculated by simple addition, but by careful accounting of combined influences that have been identified in our research analyses. The actions on the 10 levers typically have to be much bigger than you'd think, and what matters is whether they clear certain thresholds, usually in comparison with the competition. This is very important. A big move is not big because it's hard, or because the team feels stretched; it's big when it's big relative to your competition.

Who knew that whether you were in the top half or bottom half of your industry in terms of R&D spending made a 15-percentage-point difference in your chances of making it to the top quintile of the Power Curve? But it does. How many times have we seen companies shoot for a 2 percent gain in productivity, not thinking about how that moves them—or doesn't move them—against the competition? Who knew how important it was to make as many of the five moves as possible, rather than concentrate on one area for improvement, or how rare multiple moves actually are?

Is that all?

The idea that just 10 attributes can determine the odds can feel less than intuitive, even disconcerting. Surely, we are asked, other variables matter, such as talent, leadership, culture, and the deeper details of execution? There is incomplete empirical research to suggest that they would, yet, even without being able to separate these factors out, we can offer a huge improvement over what companies do today, when they mostly hope that their strategies will work. Obviously, the more than 80 percent accuracy of the model implicitly includes these other levers, because the model is built on the full empirical evidence of how companies move on the Power Curve. The other factors, such as talent and leadership, have simply not been broken out separately.

We are currently working on ways to more explicitly measure talent and incorporate it into probability estimates. For the moment, we look at the issue this way: No matter the quality of the talent base, if the strategy does not pass the thresholds of the 10 levers, it will be hard for talent to compensate for the weakness in endowment, trends, or moves.

We also looked at industry-specific Power Curves. While they are similar, their exact shape can differ. The odds will vary, too—to some extent. We have seen the average odds of making it from the middle quintiles to the top vary from 5 to 16 percent in some of the industries that we looked at in more detail. And, true, in some industries, M&A is simply not a realistic option—if a sector is already consolidated, if there are regulatory barriers, etc. We are now approaching even larger data sets with machine learning technology to see whether we can achieve another breakthrough. So, more work remains for us, and for you.

What's relevant for you and your business is that you can now know—ahead of time—your chances of succeeding with your strategy. You can know those odds precisely enough to act and see what levers matter to your own business. Because all the attributes can be measured and compared for a large sample of companies, our endowment + trends + moves model provides a true outside view of your probabilities.

What makes this a powerful tool in your hand when battling the effects of the social side of strategy is that you now have a benchmark for the quality of a strategy that's independent from subjective judgments in the strategy room. You now have an external reference point to help calibrate the likelihood of success for your strategy and, with that, a tool to change the conversation among your team.

Had such an outside view been a part of the strategy discussions at DNP or other companies with meaningful odds of dropping to the bottom quintile, those involved likely would have acted differently. When we showed the Power Curve to an insurance company in the US that was close to the top of all companies, the benchmark startled the CEO. He said: "What on Earth does that mean? Do I need to work hard just to stay there? Is there any upside left? Or can I change my industry to shift the entire curve?"

He turned to his team and asked, "Did you know this? Are you giving me strategies that will move us up on this curve? Who of you is in a business that will help me move the company?" The strategy for that company changed right then and there.

Of course, strategies live off genuine insights and new ideas. Strategy is an art. So, while you can't do much about your endowment, we'll explore in the next two chapters how you can apply some of your insights, ideas, and art to both your trends and, in particular, your moves to increase as much as possible your odds of success. You'll need to sharpen your ability to predict trends and the future moves of your competitors.

A good strategy is still hard to shape, but you can at least greatly increase your chances of understanding how close it is to a likely winner.

● ● ●

We'll now dive deeper into the roles of trends and moves, the attributes you can actually influence.

Chapter 6

The writing is on the wall

Seeing the writing on the wall is easy, but acting on it can be tough. To friend the trend, you must overcome myopia, pain-avoidance, and inertia.

I f you want to understand how important it is to get trends right, ask Cor Boonstra, former CEO of Royal Philips. He spotted a crucial one at his PolyGram unit in the late 1990s and had the courage to act on it. PolyGram was one of the world's top record labels, with a roster boasting Bob Marley, U2, and top classical artists. But Boonstra flew to New York in 1998 to meet with Goldman Sachs and sell Poly-Gram to Seagram for $10.6 billion. Why? Because Boonstra had seen proprietary research conducted by Philips' own optical storage business, showing that consumers were largely using the new recordable CD-ROM technology, which Philips co-invented, for one purpose: to copy music. The MP3 format had barely been invented, Napster was a mere gleam in Sean Parker's eye, and PolyGram was at the top of its game. But Boonstra saw the first signs of transformation and acted decisively. Within a decade, compact disc and DVD sales in the US dropped by more than 80 percent.[1]

How well did Boonstra time the sale? He nailed it. Just look at Exhibit 20, which shows that CD/DVD revenue was at its absolute peak when the PolyGram sale went through.

Exhibit 20

Disruption in the recording industry
Philips saw the writing on the wall ... and acted

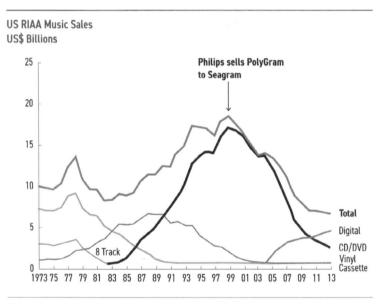

US RIAA Music Sales
US$ Billions

Source: Recording Industry Association of America

It's safe to say that most of us don't do so well in timing markets. We see trends all the time and are comfortable talking about them—what's happening in the economy, new technology innovations, what's happening in our industry, new styles of apparel, what's the matter with kids today—you name it. But ask yourself: How often do we underestimate the importance of trends, the context in which we operate, because we are accustomed to believing that we are in control? How often do we see trends but do not act fast enough on them?

Almost every strategy process pays at least some credence to trends. Boards often invite industry experts to explain their visions of the future. Or maybe your CEO visited Silicon Valley and returned inspired by the tales of innovation and technology-induced fortunes, agility, and jeans culture fantasy headquarters. Almost inevitably, ideas about blockchains, clouds, and hyperloops will seep into the strategy room, with grand visions of life a few decades from now.

In many cases, strategy teams will dutifully toil and prepare industry analyses to tick the box. "Yep, we understand the trends. Next." But, more often than not, companies don't build the capabilities or lay out the specific actions to capitalize on the trends. They rarely translate trends into practical "investable pockets" and decisively shift resources to capture the opportunities.

One of our clients got the organization to take trends seriously, but it required a real jolt. After the three of us wrote an article for the *McKinsey Quarterly* in 2011 about the *10 Timeless Tests of Strategy*,[2] that client, a large-scale global oil company, used the 10 Tests as a challenge. The board requested each business unit to prepare a brief strategy presentation, focusing on the most important choices they faced. These were given to the board, who scored each presentation using the 10 Tests. The biggest discussions ensued consistently around Test #4: Does your strategy put you ahead of trends? As a result, the company re-oriented its growth portfolio to much more explicitly invest in suitable business opportunities around the trends and micro-trends they prioritized. The gains were significant.

A very different conversation about strategy

The full mechanics, while crucial in implementation, aren't all that important here. All that's needed is to understand the outline of the levers and to see how they can lead to a very different conversation about strategy, grounded in an outside view that is far more productive than the traditional inside view that holds in the strategy room.

Again, we're not promising a crystal ball. Even if you were PCC and had a 76 percent chance of making it to the top quintile, that doesn't mean you'd have a guarantee to get there.

We naturally saw some companies that moved in ways that the model didn't suggest. A peer of PCC in the aerospace and defense industry provides a cautionary tale. It was in a growth industry, had an enviable endowment, and made apparently strong moves. The company had a 72 percent probability of lifting from the middle to the top quintile of the Power Curve over the decade we studied. Instead, it went from a $70 million economic profit to a $780 million loss, and it slid to the tail of the Power Curve.

While the company made moves, it made ones with a lower probability of success (and executed some poorly) and copped the wrong roll of the dice. A large-scale M&A strategy dramatically increased its debt without delivering returns. Low operating discipline in key aerospace and defense programs was marked by time and cost overruns. Some externalities also played a role, like lower-than-anticipated order volumes for a major product. Although a turnaround effort has improved profitability and reduced debt, the company provides a timely reminder that industry tailwinds and a strong endowment are not always enough.

On the other hand, during the decade in question the US-based hotel chain Starwood Hotels & Resorts rose to the top of the Power Curve against the odds. In an industry with a strong headwind and while holding significant debt, Starwood went from generating –$306 million in economic profit in 2000–4 to generating $332 million a decade later, outperforming the industry average of $182 million in 2010–14. Its success was driven by a counter-intuitive approach to a big move: portfolio rationalization. In this decade, Starwood made 1 acquisition (Le Méridien) and an astonishing 51 divestitures, including the sale of specific Sheraton and W luxury properties. This programmatic approach to M&A (and divestitures) supported a fundamental change in Starwood's operating model, shifting toward a brand-driven and capital-light hotel marketer and operator as opposed to a property owner. Management capitalized on Starwood's strengths, recognized the imminent headwinds and heavy debt obligations, and made a big move to beat the odds.

Despite the experience of these "despite the odds" examples, and others, our model's ability to explain 80–90 percent of the probability of movement along the Power Curve proves its merit. The exceptions often just serve to reinforce the rules. And while as humans we love heroic underdogs (and perhaps equally but less virtuously love it when big shots fail), as an investor or manager it's always smarter to go with the odds.

Tennis or badminton?

If you're going to play a racquet sport, you'd be wise to emulate tennis's Roger Federer, not badminton champion Lin Dan. Both are remarkably successful, perhaps the best ever in their games. Both are extremely marketable, with competitive instincts and personal charm. Yet no one asks, "Why doesn't Roger play badminton?" (They may instead ask, "Who is Lin Dan?") One of the reasons: A top-10 tennis player makes 10 to 20 times more than a top-10 player in any other racquet sport. No matter how great a badminton player Lin Dan is, he won't win against his "industry" disadvantage.

You, too, need to give yourself the biggest trend advantages that you can. As we've explained, the two that we've identified as most important, i.e., which way your industry and your geographies are moving, account for 25 percent of your odds of moving up or down on the Power Curve. Trends are the ground moving beneath your feet. They will move you up (or down) even before you make any other strategic moves yourself. Getting ahead of trends is easily the single most important strategic choice you have to make.

"I'm only interested in the type of trends
that result in enormous profits."

Driven by the intensity of most businesses, many tend to focus on the immediate competition but don't think much about the broader reasons for why they are moving. Maybe your gains result from your industry, not from anything particular you're doing. You might be an express courier while e-commerce is booming. Or you operate aged care facilities while the population is getting older. Maybe you're not so fortunate. Maybe you're a television broadcaster, and your audience is moving to streamed video.

Industries are escalators

Some of you may remember as children trying to beat your parents up the escalator by running up the one going down. You had to run so fast just to keep up with them floating up. Well, industries are like that—either heading up and accelerating your progress, stuck on stop-mode so it's only your effort that counts, or on a downward track, meaning you have to work hard just to stay where you are, let alone get ahead.

Of the 117 companies that jumped from the middle quintiles to the top, 85 moved with their industry (which rose at least one quintile). Only 32 moved up against a downward industry trend—a drop of at least one quintile—proving that it is possible. Of the 201 that fell from the middle quintiles to the bottom, 157 were pulled down by their industry. A firm in a top-quintile industry is five times more likely to be in the top quintile for all individual companies than one from a bottom-quintile industry (Exhibit 21).

So, it's crucial to both identify all the relevant trends and to act on them in the right timeframe. You have to make the trend your friend.

Exhibit 21

Industries are escalators
Megatrend industries help carry their members up the Power Curve

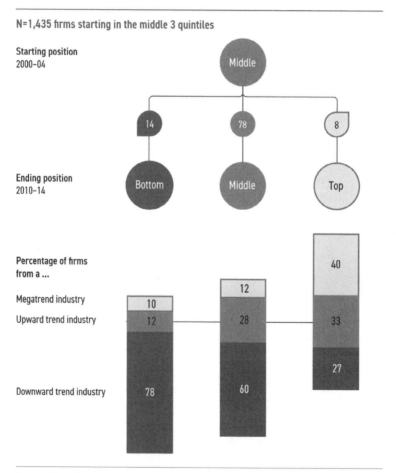

N=1,435 firms starting in the middle 3 quintiles

Source: McKinsey Corporate Performance Analytics™

As the global economy moves through cycles, as new technologies and business models emerge and older ones die, as industry structures change and new ecosystems are formed, profit pools shrink and grow and also move between industries. The results can sometimes be dramatic, requiring major action (Exhibit 22). For instance, the wireless telecom industry jumped from near the bottom of the curve 10 years ago to nearly to the top. The oil and gas industry, with the recent drop in commodity prices, went the other way in our ranking of 127 industries. Overall, the result resembles the movement among companies: Of 127 industries, 9 percent moved from the three middle quintiles up the industry Power Curve to the top over a decade.

Exhibit 22

Industries also move along their Power Curve
For example, wireless telecoms shot up the ranks, while oil and gas tumbled

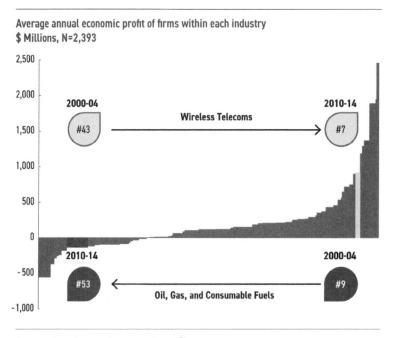

Average annual economic profit of firms within each industry
$ Millions, N=2,393

Source: McKinsey Corporate Performance Analytics™

If you find yourself with a favorable industry trend—which, as we've said, is the single most important contributor to favorable odds—then you should ride that trend as hard as you can. If, however, you find yourself with an unfavorable industry trend, you might need to seriously consider changing your industry or changing industries.

Change your industry or change industries

If you find yourself facing a disruption of the scale that Kodak did with digital photography, you have only two options: Either transform your industry, e.g., through consolidation to change its fundamental performance prospects, or decide to leave your industry to establish a new foothold in a less threatened space. Unfortunately, neither is easy.

After we presented our data at a European utility conference, three executives came up to us and said they were shocked about where their industry was located on the Power Curve. The data made it painfully clear to them that the Power Curve is highly relevant even for personal career choices, requiring people to be conscious about the position of an industry on the Power Curve and the trends that industry could expect to see.

Now, changing one's industry doesn't happen overnight, and the social side makes adapting even harder. Rarely is a business free to move from industry to industry just as the occasion demands—private equity players and venture capitalists are a notable exception. For anybody operating a company, industry-changing moves are hard—but for some of you they might be necessary.

If you're going to stay in the same industry, you might need to try finding ways to alter the dynamics of your industry to sustainably boost performance. For instance, in the beer industry in Australia, which was just a so-so performer decades ago, Lion and Foster consolidated it so thoroughly in the 1980s and 1990s that the industry became a lot more attractive for both. LAN Airways drove a new business model for airlines in South America and did extremely well. Buurtzorg Nederland has changed the home health care industry in the Netherlands and created an economic and social success story with a profoundly new and humane delivery model. What all of these have in common is that they made big, innovative moves and committed their entire companies to changing the game. They all executed strategies that dramatically altered the bases of competition in their industries and positioned themselves to capitalize on those changes.

If you can't rewrite the rules of your industry, you might have to re-position your portfolio toward new growth businesses. Strong re-allocators move more than 50 percent of their capital base to new industries over a 10-year period. Building the confidence to do so, hiring the right talent, and acquiring the necessary capabilities are tough mountains to climb.[3] For many, in the face of overwhelmingly small odds to succeed in their current industries, finding those new opportunities might be the only way to improve the odds of having a bright future.

Nearly 25 percent of the companies in our database managed to shift more than half of their capital investment over the course of a decade. Another 30 percent of companies shifted more than one-fifth.

How did they do it?

As we've said, one crucial piece is to shake free of the notion that the status quo is the baseline. Just keeping up is hard these days. The Power Curve is steep—and is getting steeper over time. Competitors are not sleeping. So, you have to throw out the notion that your industry is benign, and open the windows of the strategy room to a clear-eyed, cold-hearted outside view.

Consider changing locations, too

Although geography doesn't matter quite as much as industry, it still matters. You should assess the geographies where you operate and market your products or services for their growth potential and trends. As you can easily imagine, having exposure to high-growth geographies can also be an important factor in generating profitable growth. In general, having a granular perspective on where growth occurs is very important. A major computer manufacturer, for example, took granularity to an extraordinary degree in China. They looked at 680 major cities, grouped in 21 clusters, and prioritized cities, malls, and store locations within these malls for optimizing the return on their growth investments. Just by re-allocating sales and marketing spending, the company accelerated growth by 50 percent.

Random question: Do you know Tianjin? Chengdu? Chongqing? No?

Chongqing is a city in western China with more than 30 million (!) citizens, some of whom, more likely than not, assembled your personal ink jet/laser printer. If you don't know these cities, you probably also do not realize that more than 50 percent of global GDP growth over the next decade could be produced by 230 Chinese cities.

Over-indexing on exposure to fast-growing markets can create the obvious upside for your company's growth performance.

We found that businesses headquartered in emerging markets not only benefited from growth trends in emerging markets but also delivered stronger growth performance in developed markets. That may just be a curious side point but underscores the importance of not just focusing on your home markets. In 2012, the newly appointed CEO of Philips, Frans van Houten, launched an initiative to make China a "second home market" for the company, which resulted in accelerated growth and substantially strengthened competitiveness, especially against local competitors in China.

Even beyond the specific insights you get by understanding the relative ranking and prospects for various industries and geographies, looking at trends starts to change the dialogue in the strategy room. No longer does all credit accrue to management and all blame go to external factors that couldn't have been controlled. Now, you can actually see how much of your company's movement along the Power Curve stems from factors related to your industry and geographies and how much comes from what you and your colleagues achieved relative to the "changing of the water level." You've brought a fresh, evidence-based perspective into the conversation that can help re-frame the discussion.

Go micro

The crucial insight isn't always about mega trends or major disruption, either. One of the biggest challenges to acting on trends is the daily grind of serving your customers and responding to their needs in a timely manner. Success over the long term might simply be the accumulation of accurately understanding trends within your industry, making sure you have the flexibility to adapt and channel your resources to the best opportunities accordingly, and doing so faster than your competition.

It's picking the right geographies, the right customer segments, the right micro segments—and re-allocating resources within your current business to capitalize on differentiated growth prospects and trends. One of our authors, Sven Smit, who co-authored *Granularity of Growth* a decade ago, showed that 80 percent of the variance in growth performance of companies is explained by the choices of the markets they operate in, and M&A.[4] The PC company operating in China mentioned previously did exactly that—and executed an extremely granular approach to allocating resources ahead of growth trends.

Sir Martin Sorrell, CEO of marketing conglomerate WPP, describes how important it is to chase the opportunities within your industry:[5]

> A major reason why we've grown [. . .] is that we've tried to focus on where the growth areas are. At the moment, if your business is located in Asia and the Pacific you're going to grow faster than if it's located in Western Europe. We try to identify growth trends in our industry and our continued growth rate will be dependent on that. It will also obviously be dependent on finding the best acquisitions, but primarily it will be pushing on open doors [. . .] It doesn't matter how clever you are, if you're pushing on a closed door it's much more difficult.

Given the importance of industry position and trends, companies that best catch the waves build these perspectives into the day-to-day arsenal of how their management teams look at performance. Rather than using sporadic deep dives, often based on internal accounting data and standard market reports, you can use comprehensive analytics suites to deliver within days what was impossible to do in months just a few years ago. You can have industry-level performance comparisons and dis-aggregations, portfolio benchmarks, growth MRIs, etc., all the way to investor analytics.

The need for privileged insights

To differentiate, you need privileged insights. These come from moving from high-level trends all the way down to "investable pockets"— specific and addressable business opportunities.

Sometimes, developing the privileged insights requires investing in proprietary data. For decades, B2C companies have invested in loyalty programs (such as airline miles or retail store cards), which often provide a price discount in return for customer data. Those data allow them to derive deeper, monetizable insights. Supermarkets are now able to segment customers by several dimensions at a time (e.g., geography, demography, basket size, shop frequency, promotion participation, premium product mix, etc.). We're no longer talking about eight segments; we're talking about thousands. Supermarkets can now personalize their marketing campaigns; can tailor range by store; can understand which categories are more or less price-sensitive; can see which brands carry more loyalty; can conduct A/B testing on online channels; and so on. So, while the macro trend might say "retail is shifting toward online," it's the granular view of the customer and investable pockets that makes the shift effective.

You can also collide macro and micro insights to identify which trends are real and which are just hype or fads. In 2010, incumbent wooden shipping pallet supplier CHEP was under threat from the adoption of plastic, RFID-enabled pallets that were aggressively marketed by disruptor iGPS. Investors saw a macro trend that would mark the end of wooden pallets and encouraged CHEP to make a major investment in plastic to replace the existing pool. CHEP's micro insight was built on a detailed understanding of which customers were switching and why. CHEP recognized the underlying trend that had opened the door for the plastic threat—increased use of automation in FMCG manufacturing processes meant pallets needed to fit stricter dimensional criteria.

CHEP saw that plastic was suitable for only a niche set of customers and economically unfeasible for large scale (based on a much higher capital cost for plastic versus wood). Instead of replacing its existing $2 billion capital base and using a more expensive plastic option, CHEP responded to the underlying customer need and invested in stricter quality and repair processes. CHEP also used a dispatch algorithm that made sure that those customers that depended on the highest-quality pallets had access to them. CHEP's margin suffered slightly; iGPS went bankrupt after losing several vital customers, including PepsiCo, and was eventually picked up by a private equity firm.

Acting on the writing on the wall

Having established just how important it is to get ahead of trends, we now hit the biggest snag of them all. It is often the very same things that make companies successful that also make it hard for them to act on trends. Incumbency can make it difficult to deal with disruptions. Industry leadership can make it hard to act on the writing on the wall—but not impossible.

A decade ago, Norwegian media group Schibsted made a courageous decision: to offer classifieds—the main revenue source for its newspaper businesses—online for free. The company had already made significant Internet investments but realized that to establish a pan-European digital stronghold it had to raise the stakes. During a presentation to a prospective French partner, Schibsted executives pointed out that existing European classifieds sites had limited traffic. "The market is up for grabs," they said, "and we intend to get it." Today, over 80 percent of their earnings come from online classifieds.

About that same time, the boards of other leading newspapers were also weighing the prospect of a digital future. No doubt, like Schibsted, they even developed and debated hypothetical scenarios in which Internet start-ups siphoned off the lucrative print classified ads that the industry called its "rivers of gold." Maybe these scenarios appeared insufficiently alarming—or maybe they were too dangerous to even entertain. But very few newspapers followed Schibsted's path.

From the vantage point of today, when print media has been shattered by digital disruption, it's easy to talk about who made the right decision. Things are far murkier when one is actually in the midst of disruption's uncertain, oft-hyped early stages. In the 1980s, steel giants famously underestimated the potential of mini-mills. In the 1980s and 1990s, the personal computer put a big dent in Digital Equipment Corporation, Wang Laboratories, and other minicomputer makers. More recently, web retailers have disrupted physical ones, and Airbnb and Uber Technologies have disrupted lodging and car travel, respectively. The examples run the gamut from database software to boxed beef.

What they have in common is how often incumbents find themselves on the wrong side of a big trend. No matter how strong their balance sheets and market share going in—and sometimes because of those very factors—incumbents can't seem to hold back the tide of disrupters.

The good news is that many industries are still in the early days of disruption. Print media, travel, and lodging provide valuable illustrations of the path that increasingly more will follow. For most, it's early enough to respond.

What's the secret of those incumbents that do survive, and sometimes even thrive? One aspect surely relates to the ability to recognize and overcome the typical pattern of response (or lack thereof) that characterizes companies in the incumbent's position. This most often requires foresight and a willingness to respond boldly before it's too late, which usually means acting before it is obvious you have to do so. As Reed Hastings, the CEO of Netflix, pointed out—right as his company was making the leap from DVDs to streaming—most successful organizations fail to look for new things their customers want because they're afraid to hurt their core businesses. "Companies rarely die from moving too fast, and they frequently die from moving too slowly,"[6] he said.

We are all great strategists in hindsight. The question is what to do when you are in the middle of it all, under the real-world constraints and pressures of running a large, modern company. From an incumbent's perspective, you have to navigate four stages of a disruptive trend.

The four stages of a disruptive trend

It may help to view these stages on an S-curve (see Exhibit 23). At first, young companies struggle with uncertainty but are agile and willing to experiment. At this time, companies prize learning and optionality and work toward creating equity value based on the expectation of future earnings. The new model then needs to reach some critical mass to become a going concern. As firms mature—that is, become incumbents—mindsets and realities change. The established companies lock in routines and processes. They iron out and standardize variability amid growing organizational complexity. In the quest for efficiency, they weed out strategic options and reward executives for steady results. The measure of success is now delivery of consistent, growing cash flows in the here and now. The option-rich expectancy of future gain is replaced by the treadmill of continually escalating performance expectations.

In a disruption, the company heading toward the top of the old S-curve confronts a new business model at the bottom of a new S-curve. Creative destruction turns another cycle, but this time the shoe is on the other foot. Two primary challenges emerge.

For one, it can be hard to recognize the new S-curve, which starts with a small slope and often-unimpressive profitability, and does not

Exhibit 23

The 4 stages of a disruptive trend
When a new S-curve crashes into an old one

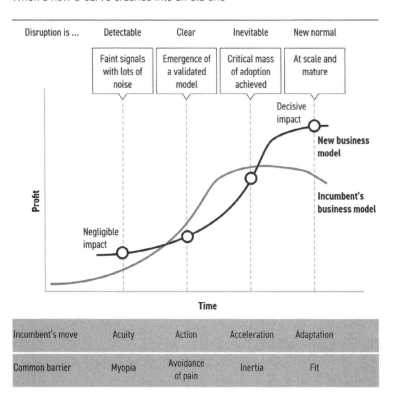

Disruption is ...	Detectable	Clear	Inevitable	New normal
	Faint signals with lots of noise	Emergence of a validated model	Critical mass of adoption achieved	At scale and mature

Incumbent's move	Acuity	Action	Acceleration	Adaptation
Common barrier	Myopia	Avoidance of pain	Inertia	Fit

catch your attention. Ray Kurzweil, the inventor, futurist, and investor, says it is difficult to recognize the early stages of exponential growth curves in the first place, as most processes in our lives evolve in a more linear manner.[7] While most companies have shown they are very good at dealing with obvious emergencies, by rapidly corralling resources and acting decisively, they struggle to deal with the slow, quiet rise of an uncertain threat that does not announce itself noisily.

The second challenge is that the same factors that help companies operate strongly at the top of an S-curve often hinder them at the bottom of a new one. Different modes of operation are required, but it's sometimes hard to do the right thing—even when you think you know what the right thing might be. New S-curves rather often also require different skill sets to succeed. The value of experience is demoted.

The simplified idea of a new S-curve crashing slow motion into an old one gives us a way to look at the problem from the incumbent's perspective and to appreciate the actual challenges each moment presents. In the first stage, the new S-curve is not yet a curve at all. In the second, the new business model gets validated, but its impact is not forceful enough to fundamentally bend the performance trajectory of the incumbent. In the third stage, the new model gains critical mass, and its impact is clearly felt. In the fourth, the new model becomes the new normal as it reaches its own maturity.

Stage one: Signals amid the noise

We already talked about how disruption hit the music business. Similarly, Spark New Zealand foresaw the deteriorating economics of its Yellow Pages business and sold its directories business in 2007 for $2.2 billion (a nine-time revenue multiple) while numerous other telecom companies held on until the businesses were nearly worthless.

The newspaper industry had no shortage of similar signals. As early as 1964, media theorist Marshall McLuhan observed that the industry's reliance on classified ads and stock-market quotes made it vulnerable: "Should an alternative source of easy access to such diverse daily information be found, the press will fold."[8] The rise of the Internet created just such a source, and start-ups like eBay opened a new way for people to list goods for sale without the use of newspaper ads. Yet Schibsted's big move to adapt in 1999 was one of the few early actions by a media company.

It's not surprising that most other publishers didn't react. At this early stage of disruption, incumbents feel barely any impact on their core businesses except in the distant periphery. They don't "need" to act. It takes rare acuity to make a pre-emptive move, likely in the face of conflicting demands from stakeholders. What's more, it can be difficult to work out which trends to ignore and which to react to.

Denial can open doors for new entrants. Aldi's successful entry into the Australian grocery market against an incumbent duopoly was, in part, enabled by the incumbents' unwillingness to acknowledge just how attractive the Aldi proposition would be to the Australian consumer. In the early days, the impact was so small—too small to push competitors into a defensive position that would sacrifice margin. You would hear language about "managing threats," but the actions suggested denial. Sixteen years later, Aldi commands market share of approximately 13 percent in Australia, which it continues to grow as it expands its store footprint.

Gaining sharper insight, and escaping the myopia of this first stage, requires incumbents to challenge their own "story" and to disrupt long-standing (and sometimes implicit) beliefs about how to make money in a given industry. As our colleagues put it in a recent article, "These governing beliefs reflect widely shared notions about customer preferences, the role of technology, regulation, cost drivers, and the basis of competition and differentiation. They are often considered inviolable—until someone comes along to violate them."[9]

The process of reframing these governing beliefs involves identifying an industry's foremost notion about value creation and then turning it on its head to find new forms and mechanisms for creating value.

The social side of strategy will, as usual, complicate the reframing. People have become accustomed to the old way of thinking, and changing mindsets is hard. Many also have businesses that are making a lot of money based on the old S-curve and, in the battle for resources, might—at least quietly—stem attempts to shift toward a new one.

The traditionalists' arguments will be especially persuasive in the early stages, before the attractiveness of the transition becomes clear.

As personal-computer pioneer Alan Kay used to say, "Everybody likes change, except for the change part."

Stage two: Change takes hold

The trend is now clear. The core technological and economic drivers have been validated. At this point, it's essential for established companies to commit to nurturing new initiatives so that they can establish footholds in the new sphere. More important, they need to ensure that new ventures have autonomy from the core business, even if the goals of the two operations conflict. The idea is to act before one has to.

But with disruption's impact still not big enough to dampen earnings momentum, motivation is often missing. Even as online classifieds for cars and real estate began to take off and Craigslist gained momentum, most newspaper publishers lacked a sense of urgency because their own market shares remained largely unaffected. And it's not like the new players were making millions (yet). There was no performance envy.

But Schibsted did find the necessary motivation. "When the dot-com bubble burst, we continued to invest, in spite of the fact that we didn't know how we were going to make money online," recalls CEO Kjell Aamot. "We also allowed the new products to compete with the old products." Offering free online classifieds directly cannibalized its newspaper business, but Schibsted was willing to take the risk. The company didn't just act; it acted radically.

Microsoft made a similarly radical shift after then-CEO Bill Gates took one of his "think weeks" in 1995 and realized that the company was greatly underestimating the importance of the Internet. He returned with his famous "Internet memo" and fundamentally reoriented the company, killing some projects, re-allocating resources to others, and launching still more.

Now, let's openly acknowledge how hard it is for a company's leaders to commit to supporting experimental ventures when the business is climbing the S-curve. Not many companies have a Bill Gates lying around. When Netflix disrupted itself in 2011 by shifting focus from DVDs to streaming, its share price dropped by 80 percent. Few boards and investors can handle that kind of pain when the near-term need is debatable. The vague longer-term threat just doesn't seem as dangerous as the immediate hardship. After all, incumbents have existing revenue streams to protect—start-ups only have upside to capture. Additionally, management teams are more comfortable developing strategies for businesses they know how to operate, and are naturally reluctant to enter a new game with rules they don't understand. In other words, the social side of strategy rules again.

The upshot: Most incumbents dabble, making small investments that won't flatten their current S-curve and that guard against cannibalization. Usually, incumbents focus too heavily on finding synergies (always looking for efficiency) rather than fostering radical experimentation. The illusion that this dabbling is getting you into the game is all too tempting to believe. Many newspapers built online add-ons to their classified businesses, but few were willing to risk cannibalizing the traditional revenue streams, which at this point were still far bigger and more profitable. And remember, at this time, Schibsted had not yet been rewarded for its early action: Its results looked pretty similar to its peers.

In time, of course, bolder action becomes necessary, and executives must commit to nurturing potentially dilutive and small next-horizon businesses in a pipeline of initiatives. Managing such a portfolio requires high tolerance for ambiguity, and it requires executives to adapt to shifting conditions, both inside and outside the company, even as the aspiration to deliver favorable outcomes for shareholders remains constant. The difficulty is the tendency to protect the core because of short-term financial incentives and emotional ties that inhibit a shift to the periphery.

No small part of the challenge is to accept that the previous status quo is no longer the baseline. The future success of grocery retailer Aldi's low-price model was visible while Aldi was still nascent. Yet many incumbent supermarkets chose to avoid the near-term pain of sharpening entry price points and improving their private-label brands. In hindsight, those moves cleared the way for Aldi's continued strong growth across three continents.

Stage three: The inevitable transformation

By now, the future is pounding on the door. The new model has proved superior to the old, at least for some critical mass of adopters, and the industry is in motion. At this stage of disruption, to accelerate its own transformation, the incumbent's challenge lies in aggressively shifting resources to the new, self-competing ventures it nurtured in stage two. Think of the change as treating new businesses like venture-capital investments that only pay off if they scale rapidly, while the old ones are subject to a private-equity-style workout.

Making this tough shift requires overcoming the inertia that can afflict companies even in the best of times. As we've seen, the social side of strategy almost guarantees a peanut-butter approach to allocating resources, making a sharp reorientation hard to pull off.

The hardest stage

In fact, our experience suggests stage three is the hardest one for incumbents to navigate. As company performance starts to suffer, tightening up budgets, established companies naturally tend to cut back even further on peripheral activities while focusing on the core. The top decision makers, who usually come from the biggest business centers, resist having their still-profitable (though more sluggishly growing) domains starved of resources in favor of unproven upstarts. As a result, leadership often under-invests in new initiatives and imposes high performance hurdles on them. Legacy businesses continue to receive the lion's share of resources. By this time, the very forces causing pressure in the core make the business even less willing and able to address those forces. Under the influence of the social side of strategy, the reflex to conserve resources kicks in just when you most need to aggressively re-allocate and invest.

Boards play a significant role. Far too often, boards are unwilling (or unable) to change their view of baseline performance, further exacerbating the problem. Often, a board's (understandable) reaction to reduced performance is to push management even harder to achieve ambitious goals within the current model, ignoring the need for a more fundamental change. This only worsens problems in the future.

Further complicating matters, incumbents with initially strong positions can take false comfort at this stage, because the weaker players in the industry get hit hardest first. The narrative that "it is not happening to us" is all too tempting to believe. The key is to closely monitor the underlying drivers and not just use hindsight based on financial outcomes. The tale says, "I don't have to outrun the bear . . . I just have to outrun you," but, when it comes to disruption, that strategy merely buys time. The bear will keep running, and it will get to you, too.

Even when the course is reasonably clear, getting the team moving in a new direction can be hard. When an Asian high-tech manufacturer diversified into green energy, not a single member of the top team wanted to lead the business. The company brought in an outsider, but he was never able to marshal enough resources from the core business.

The strategy was right, but the lack of a strong leader led to failure and a $10 million write-off just a few years later. Similarly, an Australian bank wanted to expand into Indonesia to catch the trend of consumer growth and digital there. Not a single member of the top team raised his or her hand when asked for volunteers to build this growth pillar. The company abandoned the plans right then and there.

To generate the acceleration needed at this stage of the game, incumbents must embark on a courageous and unremitting re-allocation of resources from the old to the new model and show a willingness to run new businesses differently (and often separately) from the old ones. Perhaps nothing underlines this point more than Axel Springer's 2013 divestment of some of its strongest legacy print media products, which accounted for about 15 percent of its sales, to Germany's number three print media player, Funke Mediengruppe. These products, such as *The Berliner Morgenpost*, owned by Axel Springer since 1959, were previously a core part of the corporate DNA and emblems of its journalistic culture. But no more. Axel Springer realized that the future value of the business was not just about continuation of today's earnings but rather relied on the creation of a new economic engine. The German media company was "a mere Internet midget," according to *Financial Times Deutschland*, until it leapt into action in 2005.[10] It went on a shopping spree, acquiring 67 digital properties and launching 90 initiatives of its own by 2013. Most important was choosing a new area to expand into—online classifieds, which were both high-margin and high-growth—and doubling down on it. The lesson from Axel Springer, like Schibsted, is that incumbents can win even with a late start, provided that they throw themselves in wholly. Today, over 80 percent of Axel Springer's EBITDA is derived from digital.

When incumbents lack the in-house capability to build new businesses, they must look to acquire them instead. Here the challenge is to time acquisitions somewhere between where the business model is proved and where valuations become too high—all while making sure the incumbent is a "natural best owner" of the businesses it acquires. Examples of this approach in the financial sector include BBVA's acquisition of Simple and Capital One's acquisition of the design firm Adaptive Path.

Stage four: Adapting to the new normal

In this late stage, the disruption has reached a point where companies have no choice but to accept reality: The industry has fundamentally changed. For incumbents, their cost base isn't in line with the new (likely much shallower) profit pools, their earnings are caving in, and they find themselves poorly positioned to take a strong market position.

This is where print media is now. The classifieds' "rivers of gold" have dried up, making survival the first priority and growth the second. In 2013, the CEO of Australian media company Fairfax Media told the International News Media Association World Congress, "We know that at some time in the future, we will be predominantly digital or digital-only in our metropolitan markets."[11] True, some legacy mastheads have created powerful online news properties with high traffic, but display advertising and paywalls alone are for the most part not enough to generate a thriving revenue line, and social aggregation sites are continuing to drive unbundling. Typical media firms have had to undertake the multiple painful waves of restructuring and consolidation that may be needed while they seed growth and look for ways to monetize their brands.

For the incumbents that, like Axel Springer and Schibsted, have made the leap, the adaptation phase brings new challenges. They are now majority-digital businesses fully exposed to the volatility and pace that come with the territory. Rather than resting on their laurels, they adapt through continual self-disruption. Think of Facebook upending its business model in 2013 to go "mobile first," or China's Tencent letting the mobile-based Wechat cannibalize its already dominant QQ desktop social media platform. You can't be satisfied with the first pivot; you have to be prepared to keep pivoting.

In some cases, incumbents' capabilities are so highly tied to the old business model that rebirth through restructuring is unlikely to work, and an exit is the best way to preserve value. Eastman Kodak Company, for example, may have been better off leaving the photography business much faster, because its numerous strategies all failed to save it. When a business is built on a legacy technology that is categorically different from the new standard, even perfect foresight of the demise of film or CDs would not have solved the core problem that the digital replacement is fundamentally less profitable.

The social side of strategy can, again, complicate the shift. Unlike Axel Springer, most find it hard to part with a business that is so identified with their history. When a very senior, proud, and successful executive has run a business for so long, it's hard for the CEO to pull resources away from them, even when the business is threatened. Boards and management teams find it hard to let go of old ideas, including assumptions about profitability. In many companies, there is nothing more sacred than the business they originally were built around.

The challenge is to adapt and structurally realign cost bases to the new reality of profit pools and accept that the "new normal" likely includes far fewer "rivers of gold."

● ● ●

While getting trends right is hard, there is good news in the next chapter: We lay out what we found about the combinations of big moves that can also help you reposition your business ahead of trends.

It's taken a bit of a journey, but we're now set up for the most consequential discussion. You now have an outside view that helps you benchmark your performance, think about your odds of achieving a significant success, and understand the endowment you began with and the trends that are affecting you.

You can now ask the most important question: What are my big moves?

"As a tribute to all the people who led this company before me . . . let's play it safe."

Chapter 7

Making the right (big) moves

Five big moves make all the difference in shifting your odds. Big moves sound scary, but they are actually the safest bet. They are best done by purposefully making a series of smaller steps over time.

On page 37 of the strategy discussion, you lost sight of what's important and what's not. You were listening to long lists of things that need to get done to grow market share, to win the next big account, to improve margin. At the outset of the discussion in the strategy room, you might have started talking about the big choices, but that was weeks earlier. Now, you are buried in the detail of the first-year operating budget of your 5-year strategic plan. Everything is becoming incremental.

Most of us have been ground down in a situation like that, and, as our research shows—confirming what we've sensed all along—incremental doesn't get companies very far. In fact, incremental moves increase the risk of underperformance.

To keep us away from incrementalism and focused on what matters, we'll describe in this chapter the five big moves that play by far the most significant role in determining your odds of success. The list is short, so you can keep the conversation in the strategy room focused on it, heading off those page 37 woes and giving yourself a shot at real success.

You begin with your endowment—what you have been given, based on your size, your debt level, and your investment in R&D. You also operate within the context of trends, which are also largely out of your control initially but which you can influence by adapting your resource allocation to catch the right waves. But moves are where the action is. They're more within your control, the things you do. Moves put your money where your mouth is. Moves are collectively the strongest determinants of success—and that's empowering.

So, we'll go through the five big moves that we briefly outlined before: programmatic M&A and divestitures, resource re-allocation, capital expenditure, productivity improvement, and differentiation improvement. Every CEO has most or all of them on the to-do list—who isn't interested in better productivity, or investing in growth opportunities?

However, it's important to keep in mind that the five big moves:

- Matter, because **they predict success** more than any others
- **Need to be pulled hard** enough to make a difference to your odds of climbing the Power Curve
- Are most **effective when combined**—and the worse your endowment or trends, the more moves you need to make

What surprises most business leaders we talk to is just *how big* a big move really needs to be. Over the many decades of interacting with and advising business leaders around the world, we've so often seen teams start with big ambitions, only to have them drain away. Why is it so hard to make big moves, moves that change the odds? As we've said before, just because a move feels big, is hard to do, or takes a lot of resources, this does not mean it's a "big" move. You need an external reference point: It has to be big versus what the rest of the world is doing. You have to take the outside view; don't get stuck inside.

Big moves feel scary. Risk aversion is human and permeates all parts of many organizations. The CEO may be trying to deliver on the quarter rather than thinking a decade ahead: "My legacy matters. I won't mess it up with this acquisition." Elsewhere, managers are not ready to take risks with new initiatives. One might be concerned about not achieving an ambitious target—or similar career-limiting actions. Another might fear neglecting other priorities, and thus spreads effort too widely and thinly. Or, perhaps a founder/chairman has made billions and simply doesn't want to take perceived risks that would put his fortunes or social status in peril. You might think that, once an entrepreneur, always an entrepreneur, but that's not always the case. We have seen more than once successful entrepreneurs turn cautious and push their teams into an incremental, "Let's make next year just a bit better than this year." For many, entrepreneurship is great—as long as they're not the ones taking the career risk.

In many situations, you might end up with a finger-pointing exercise. The CEO of a consumer business in India blamed the front line—"We have the right strategy, but my team does not execute." Others say there's something wrong with the strategy, or with the CEO, or with both. Most often, though, unexpected "one-time effects" are blamed for not progressing on the Power Curve.

"WHO'S GOT A BOLD PLAN THAT WILL TOTALLY CHANGE THE GAME IN OUR INDUSTRY AND WON'T PISS ME OFF?"

Big moves are essential

We're sympathetic to all these problems—we recognize our own humanity in many of them. But our research found that big moves are essential if you're to improve your chances of moving up the Power Curve. So, it isn't enough to just understand that big moves have historically been hard. We have to escape the past and get to a place where big moves become possible, even encouraged.

Fortunately, once you open the windows of the strategy room and bring in the outside view, you can use these empirics and what we learn from them to change the game. Not because they are another set of numbers, but because calibrating and benchmarking strategies allows you to change the dialogue in the room. You have compelling arguments—based on clear evidence—that big moves do matter.

As we've seen, companies in the middle quintiles of the Power Curve have an 8 percent chance of reaching the top quintile over a decade. Making one or two big moves, i.e., pulling one or two of the five levers hard enough to matter, more than doubles those odds to 17 percent. Three big moves boost these odds to 47 percent —irresistible odds, as we will see later for the likes of BASF, Konica Minolta, and Asahi, which all succeeded in making multiple big moves to scale the Power Curve. Companies that made three or more big moves were six times more likely to jump from the middle quintile to the top.

Unfortunately, it is rare that companies will make more than a single big move. Of all the companies that started in the middle of the Power Curve, roughly 40 percent didn't make any big moves at all over the 10-year period. Another nearly 40 percent only made one (Exhibit 24). There's actually more action from the bottom group, highlighting that weak performance is a catalyst for change.

There were 60 companies in our research that pulled four or five levers in the period 2000–4 to 2010–14. Within this group of 60 strong movers, 40 were upwardly mobile, and there were no downwardly mobile companies. Just take a second to reflect on that. Not a single company that pulled four or five levers slid down on the Power Curve. If that's not getting you thinking, we don't know what would.

Exhibit 24

Big moves are rare but valuable

Only 23% of middle-tier firms made 2 or more big moves

Big moves made, 2000–04 to 2010–14

Moves	All firms N=879[1]	Firms in middle tier, 2000–04 N=350[1]	Odds of reaching the top from the middle Overall subset odds, 15%
0	18.8%	39.1%	8
1	29.6%	38.0%	17
2	29.4%	18.0%	16
3	15.1%	4.2%	40
4	5.8%	0.5%	100
5	1.0%	0%	NA

1 Firms with data for at least 4 of 5 moves

Source: McKinsey Corporate Performance Analytics™

Of the 60 companies that pulled four or five levers, two moved from middle to top, and 22 made the more impressive leap from bottom quintile to top quintile (Exhibit 25).

Included in that group are: heavy equipment manufacturer Komatsu, hotel operator Starwood Hotels, media conglomerates Disney and 21st Century Fox, Canadian telco Telus, aerospace and defense suppliers Rolls Royce Holdings, Precision Castparts, Harris Corp., Raytheon, and Northrop Grumman, and other well-known names including Japan Airlines, Goodyear, and Mitsubishi Electric. Growing economic profit is not always accompanied by growing sales; for example, Goodyear grew their profit margins while experiencing a top-line decline in the latter half of the period.

Exhibit 25

Big movers
24 firms went to the top with 4 or more big moves

Name	Industry	Country	Start Category	End Category
Agilent Technologies Inc	Life Sciences Tools & Services	USA	Bottom	Top
Bayer AG	Pharmaceuticals	Germany	Bottom	Top
BCE Inc	Diversified Telco Services	Canada	Bottom	Top
Citic Ltd	Industrial Conglomerates	Hong Kong	Bottom	Top
Continental AG	Auto Components	Germany	Bottom	Top
Corning Inc	Elec. Equip., Inst. & Components	USA	Bottom	Top
DirecTV	Media	USA	Bottom	Top
Disney (Walt) Co	Media	USA	Bottom	Top
Goodyear Tire & Rubber	Auto Components	USA	Bottom	Top
Halliburton Co	Energy Equipment & Services	USA	Bottom	Top
Harris Corp	Communications Equipment	USA	Middle	Top
Japan Airlines Co Ltd	Airlines	Japan	Bottom	Top
Komatsu Ltd	Machinery	Japan	Bottom	Top
Mitsubishi Electric Corp	Electrical Equipment	Japan	Bottom	Top
Monsanto Co	Chemicals	USA	Bottom	Top
Northrop Grumman Corp	Aerospace & Defense	USA	Bottom	Top
Precision Castparts Corp	Aerospace & Defense	USA	Middle	Top
Raytheon Co	Aerospace & Defense	USA	Bottom	Top
Rogers Communications	Wireless Telco Services	Canada	Bottom	Top
Rolls-Royce Hldgs Plc	Aerospace & Defense	UK	Bottom	Top
Schlumberger Ltd	Energy Equipment & Services	USA	Bottom	Top
Starwood Hotels & Resorts	Hotels, Restaurants & Leisure	USA	Bottom	Top
Telus Corp	Diversified Telco Services	Canada	Bottom	Top
Twenty-First Century Fox	Media	USA	Bottom	Top

Source: McKinsey Corporate Performance Analytics™

Communications technology company Harris made four of the five big moves over the decade: programmatic mergers, acquisitions, and divestitures (M&A&D), dynamic resource re-allocation, productivity improvement in terms of labor and overhead, and differentiation with gross margin expansion. Check out their mobility dashboard in Exhibit 26. Harris also benefited from an industry megatrend, low debt, and high R&D spending in the past. That's seven boxes ticked out of the 10 mobility attributes, which is why Harris had an 80 percent probability of moving from the middle to the top of the Power Curve. The move produced a 13 percent CAGR in total shareholder return over the decade.

Exhibit 26

Harris' mobility dashboard

Pulling 4 big moves with a positive industry trend took Harris to the top

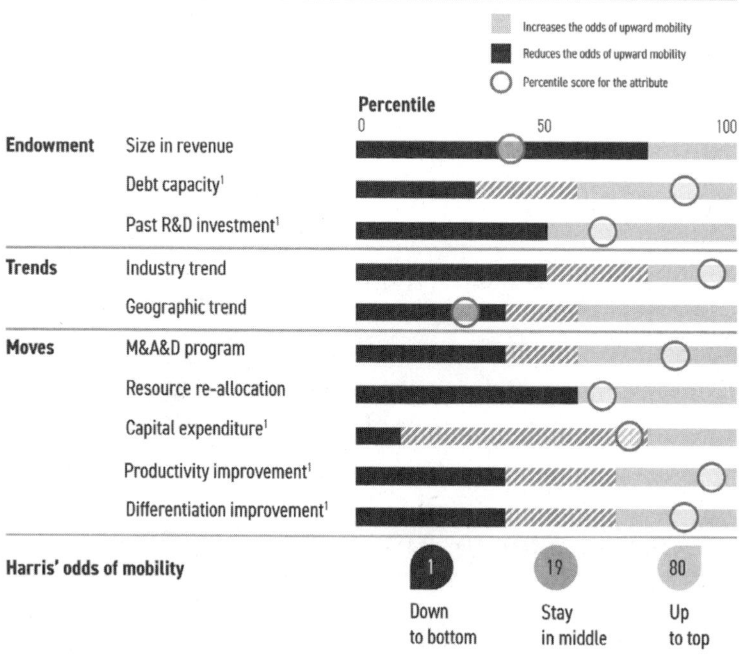

1 Relative to industry

Source: McKinsey Strategy Practice (Beating the Odds model v.18.3) and Corporate Performance Analytics™

Corning's story

Corning pulled all five of the big moves over the 10-year period and leapt from bottom to top. Their sales productivity went up by 80 percent; gross margin expanded by 14 percent; the ratio of SG&A to sales fell by 30 percent. Corning spent $14 billion on capex and net $3.2 billion on acquisitions (12 acquisitions and 9 divestments). Despite starting in the bottom quintile, Corning gave itself a 78 percent chance of at least moving to the middle and fully a 49 percent chance of reaching the top quintile.

Corning's average annual economic profit improved by around $1.7 billion. And, importantly, 90 percent of the improvement in Corning's economic profit was attributable to the company—not the market, not the industry, but to Corning's big moves.

Corning's story is more fascinating than just the numbers. For a company with a long and proud history—having made the glass encasing Thomas Edison's lightbulb, windows for the Apollo lunar landings, and the first fiber-optic cable—consider the challenges that Corning faced in the early 2000s. Heavily invested in telecommunications, Corning was hit hard by the bursting of the dot-com bubble. Revenue halved, profits turned into heavy losses, and the share price plummeted 99 percent from its peak in September 2000 to its low in October 2002.

Corning's approach to recovery was a balance of scaling back the portfolio and scrutinizing the cost base, but also maintaining investment in R&D and long-term growth—the latter very difficult under the short-term pressure of shareholders. Corning produced an amazing turnaround based on big moves.

Here is a detailed look at our five big moves and why they matter so much, with a few examples sprinkled in along the way.

Programmatic M&A and divestitures

The myth that 75 percent of all mergers fail has long been dispelled. It was based on a statistic related to "announcement day effect" that failed to capture the reality of corporate value creation (not to mention the many smaller deals that don't get announced but cumulatively matter a lot). M&A does work as a growth lever. But success depends very much on the type of M&A program a company is running.[1]

The path that holds the most promise is programmatic M&A. Our research found that the most successful style of M&A executes on average at least one deal per year in a program that cumulatively amounts to more than 30 percent of market capitalization over 10 years, with no single deal being more than 30 percent of market cap. Companies that meet this standard on M&A have cleared the threshold and made a big move.

The findings make sense, considering that M&A requires mastery of capabilities through repeated deals. M&A requires a set of capabilities that are built over time, as a result of practice. Companies that execute programmatic M&A over years, often decades, become true masters of the art of identifying, negotiating, and integrating acquisitions.

Companies that do very few deals struggle to execute well the few they do. Practice makes perfect—the adage holds. Our research has shown that infrequent, large deals tend to hurt value creation.

Corning shows the value of this move. At all times, they seek to maintain a strong M&A pipeline that is about 5 to 10 times their annual target for increasing revenue through acquisitions. Corning understands that doing three deals a year means it has to do due diligence on 20 companies and submit five bids.

Axel Springer and WPP also show the value of programmatic M&A, as we described in a bit of detail in the section on the importance of recognizing and acting on trends.

Axel Springer, the giant German publisher, made a decisive move from print to digital by making 67 mostly small acquisitions between 2006 and 2012, while launching 90 publications organically and divesting itself of eight. The company's disciplined approach to M&A repositioned it solidly for the digital age and led to a 10 percent CAGR in total shareholder return over the decade.

While the company had lost some momentum as of the writing of this book, global marketing powerhouse WPP is a strong example of programmatic M&A. In the early days, following WPP's pivot from industrial manufacturing to marketing services, major acquisitions were the fastest way to achieve scale in its new industry. WPP acquired JWT for $566 million in 1987 and Ogilvy for $864 million in 1989. Those acquisitions were big enough that WPP admits stretching their balance sheet and risking distress. However, since then, WPP has practiced programmatic M&A and made it one of the company's strongest muscles. Over the 10-year sample period, WPP made 271 acquisitions (that's more than 1 per fortnight), which was 60 percent more transactions than the next busiest acquirer, Alphabet Inc. WPP began the period in the middle of the Power Curve, with average economic profit of $8 million, but ended with a top-quintile-worthy $677 million. The company saw an 11 percent CAGR in total shareholder return over the decade.

The repetition of M&A will help you get past the curse of intro-spection. It also will help strengthen the capabilities of your business. M&A and post-merger integration programs are not innate talents; they are mastery acquired by doing them over and over again.

Active resource re-allocation

Peanut butter can taste great on a sandwich, but this is not about taste, and spreading peanut butter doesn't work for allocating resources—capital, operating expenses, and talent—to the most important growth opportunities across the company. Spreading resources evenly provides too much to those units that aren't going to make a big move—or can't—while depriving those one or two that could turn into huge opportunities. The social side of strategy creates peanut butter tendencies and causes inertia about those allo-cation decisions.

"With the proper budgetary allocations you'll be
able to see our economic profit from space."

The needed re-allocation isn't just movement between industries, geographies, operating segments, business units, projects, products, or customer groups; it's all of the above. Breaking inertia, freeing up resources from under-performing units, and shifting them to over-performing units creates value at all levels irrespective of how you define those units. The problem, of course, is that in a world of finite resources, re-allocating resources to one inevitably requires deallocating resources from another—and this is where the friction and inertia set in.

Here's a fact that will be near and dear to every CEO's heart: At a time when average CEO tenures are rapidly dropping, CEOs who aggressively move in their first few years to re-allocate resources to new growth spaces tend to keep their jobs longer than their more reluctant peers.[2]

Dynamic re-allocation creates value. The analytics are unambiguous. Companies that shift more than 50 percent of their capital expenditure across business units over 10 years create 50 percent more value over that period than companies that move resources at a slower clip. Again, just shifting some isn't enough. You have to clear that 50 percent threshold to get the big boost in your odds of reaching the top quintile.

Reckitt Benckiser made a big move when the British consumer goods company decided to rearticulate priorities and, within 2 weeks, increased the resources allocated to a promising area by a factor of 2½. At Virgin, Richard Branson has been the very model of resource re-allocation while building a personal fortune of some $5 billion. He started in record stores, moved to music, then to airlines—his Virgin Group now controls more than 400 companies and continues its relentless re-allocation of resources to promising opportunities in renewable fuels, healthcare, and even space travel and Elon Musk's Hyperloop venture.

Well before agreeing to sell $52.4 billion of assets to Walt Disney in late 2017, 21st Century Fox migrated its resource allocation to support the evolution of media consumption habits. Fox shifted away from traditional print media to focus on filmed content and broadcasting. Back in 2001, 50 percent of News Corp.'s operating income came from print media, and only 6 percent from cable network programming; after spinning off its print assets and rebranding, 21st Century Fox made two-thirds of its operating income from cable and none from print. Total shareholder return grew at a 10 percent CAGR over the decade.

When Frans van Houten became Philips' CEO in 2011, the company began divesting itself of legacy assets, including its TV and audio businesses. After this portfolio restructuring, Philips succeeded at reinvigorating its growth engine by re-allocating resources to more promising businesses (oral care and healthcare were two priorities) and geographies. Philips started, for example, managing performance and resource allocations at the level of more than 340 business-market combinations, such as power toothbrushes in China and respiratory care in Germany. That led to an acceleration of growth, with the consumer business moving from the company's worst-performing segment to its best-performing one within 5 years.

Danaher has practiced active resource re-allocation throughout its long history, and, accordingly, the company has continually innovated. For what was originally a real estate investment trust, Danaher now boasts a wide portfolio of science, technology, and manufacturing companies across life sciences, diagnostics, environmental & applied solutions, and dental (although these segments are periodically reviewed and re-cut to avoid allocation inertia).

Danaher has made sure its structure and processes create resource liquidity to chase the best opportunities at any point in time. Like a private equity firm, the management team spends half of their time focused on resource re-allocation, including M&A opportunities, organic investments, and divestments. One fundamental process sitting behind Danaher's success is the Danaher Business System, or DBS. The system draws on concepts like lean manufacturing and the Kaizen philosophy of continuous improvement. DBS is used to identify the best investment opportunities, drive operational improvements to free up resources, and create world-class capabilities in the businesses Danaher acquires.[3]

Danaher was a top-quintile company throughout our research, but big moves, such as dynamic resource re-allocation, business model differentiation, and programmatic M&A, lifted its economic profit by an additional $512 million, placing it even higher on the Power Curve. Total shareholder return grew at a 12 percent CAGR over the decade.

Exhibit 27 shows just how aggressively Danaher re-allocated capital.

Exhibit 27

Danaher's dynamic resource re-allocation
Danaher moved capex aggressively from old to new fields

Share of capex by business unit, percent

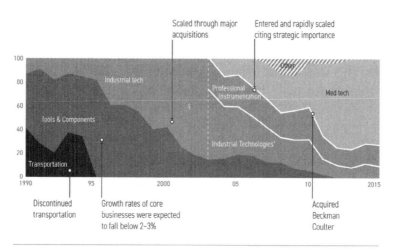

1 The segment was split in 2003 into Professional Instrumentation and Industrial Technologies

Source: Compusat; Annual reports

Re-allocation is not just limited to capex across segments. Re-allocation within segments is important, too, and so is re-allocation of operating expenses. A diversified North American industrial conglomerate looked at R&D and sales expenditure by product line within its US market segments. It used an analytical process to find products that it would classify as "Sustain"—those that are profitable but not necessarily the most attractive, where the main goal is sustaining current profitability rather than pursuing growth. The process used several filters to find the Sustain products: Was the product dilutive to margin, was it dilutive to growth, was it an attractive market, did the company have strategic advantage in that market, was the product material enough to free up meaningful resources, and was the product sufficiently independent from the rest of the portfolio (to minimize adverse spill-over from reduced allocation)? The company found 15 of its 80 products were Sustain products and, from them, identified

$35–45 million of R&D and sales spending that could be freed up and re-allocated, representing approximately 10 percent of the division's allocation.

To re-allocate, you have to de-allocate

Now, that might all sound great, but re-allocating resources is often not so easy. If you don't build a cushy balance sheet, the showstopper when trying to re-allocate resources happens typically on October 31, after the first round of the annual planning process, when it is evident that there are no resources available to be re-allocated. You may also have trouble when a strategically important M&A comes along and you just don't have the resources.

Taking resources away from a unit on the spur of the moment is much harder than handing out resources, so you need to plan ahead. Cut resources in January to have flexibility to hand out resources in August.

Often, it turns out to be much easier to identify the likely losers than the likely winners—most executives we know usually have little trouble agreeing which businesses will fail (unless they're the ones running them). So, you can cut costs at some units. You can also raise capital and sell assets or businesses to stockpile resources.

The social side of strategy makes resource allocations sticky. Inertia matters—a lot—and so do our organizational silos. We often don't look at all our resources in their proper context and see how they can be shared or moved. The inside view keeps getting tighter and tighter as you go down the company structure.

Strong capital programs

The third big move is to expand faster than the industry. Pulling the capex lever turns into a big move when your capex/sales ratio exceeds 1.7 times the industry median for at least 10 years.

Successful capital programs manage a pipeline: making sure you aren't just investing in options that you know are "in the money"; making sure you're investing in some riskier, medium-term options for the company and some longer-term, even-higher-risk options; making sure your pipeline of investments is full.

Taiwanese semiconductor manufacturer TSMC succeeded by going anti-cyclical when the Internet bubble burst and demand for semiconductors dropped sharply. TSMC bought mission-critical equipment at the trough of the crisis and was ready for the demand as soon as it came back. TSMC had been in a head-to-head race before the crisis but pulled clear of the competition after it ended because of its through-cycle investment strategy. That laid the foundation for establishing technology leadership in subsequent years, making TSMC one of the largest and most successful semiconductor manufacturing pure plays in the world. The company's total shareholder return grew at a 15 percent CAGR over the decade.

Canadian National Railway moved to the top quintile with a significant capex program. Over the period 2005 to 2014, CN invested more than C$17 billion in capex, a staggering 85 percent of the capital base that it had in 2004. Railroads are a capital-intensive business, and more than half of CN's investment went into track infrastructure. However, the investment wasn't just about sprawling farther and wider; the route-miles of CN's network hardly changed over the decade. No, most of the track capex went into repairs and upgrades that would open capacity and improve operational efficiency of the network; for example, building longer sidings to support longer trains. The program was associated with an 18 percent CAGR in total shareholder return over the decade—making the formerly state-owned CN one of the most successful privatizations ever.

For Fortescue Metals, the opportunity was in constructing its Pilbara mines while the iron ore price supported it—and it went on to build a major global force in mining from nothing. For Patrick Stevedores, the opportunity was replacing labor with automation, which lifted throughput, reduced costs, improved safety, and won back some bargaining power over unions.

There must, of course, be real discipline and robust investment processes. If a project doesn't generate returns at least equal to the cost of capital, it's actually destroying value for shareholders. Again, this is one of the reasons why we use economic profit—after capital charges have been deducted—as our measure of financial performance for observing the Power Curve.

Caution on capex

Capex in itself doesn't make a strategy successful. Additional capacity is just excess capacity unless there is underlying demand for it. Spending capex can be a positive or a negative depending on whether it is based on privileged assets or insights. This is different than the other big moves, which are clearly asymmetric: They increase the odds of moving up while simultaneously decreasing the risk of sliding down. Capex is more like an amplifier, pushing you faster in either direction.

Santos is a cautionary example. The Australian gas company, whose contracts tend to be linked to oil, pulled the capex lever hard and invested heavily over 2011 to 2014 as it developed new projects and expanded its existing Cooper Basin asset. The crude oil price had rallied since the financial crisis and found some relative stability between $100 and $120 per barrel. Over the 4 years Santos invested approximately $10 billion in capex, which, until the projects became operational, were extremely costly and a heavy drag on economic profit. Santos slid to the bottom quintile of the Power Curve during this heavy period of investment. And maybe that would have been okay, because big projects take time to operate and bear fruit, but then the oil price halved in 2015—and it hasn't recovered. Not surprisingly, Santos found it very challenging to deal with the subsequent cash-flow problems.

Distinctive productivity improvement

Productivity programs are a management favorite. They are mostly under management control, a lever that can be pulled with relative certainty. Companies like Toyota made their fortunes based on productivity-led advantages. However, everybody does these programs, so do they really move the needle, or do they help to just keep up with the industry?

Productivity programs only make a real difference once you clear a high threshold. You have to deliver 25 percent more productivity improvement than your industry median over a 10-year period. If your industry improves productivity at 2 percent per year, your program would need to consistently deliver above 2.5 percent per year. Sounds like not too much, but very few companies manage to do 25 percent better than the rest of the industry, every year, over a 10-year period.

Pulling this lever hard normally requires extraordinary means and efforts. In our experience, Six Sigma, Lean, and other methodologies have contributed enormously over the last few decades to extraordinary productivity improvements.[4] However, even more important than the methodology is the productivity program itself. Being able to force the entire organization into consistently driving productivity over time, and capturing the bottom-line impact, are real differentiators. Toyota succeeded in such a big way primarily by establishing a company-wide culture of continuous productivity improvement that is deeply embedded and constantly reinforced.

"YOUR PERFORMANCE LEVER SEEMS TO BE STUCK."

Running fast and getting nowhere

What struck us, though, is that many companies do feel like they're running rather fast but getting nowhere—relative to competition. All too often, the hard work on productivity is given away in pricing or, worse, lost when other parts of the organization absorb the gains—the dreaded "German sausage effect": You squeeze on one end, and the fat sloshes to the other end.

Car companies invested heavily to shorten the product lifecycle of models, from 12 years, to 7 years, to 5, and to even faster "refresh" rates—but everyone did so, so no one gained a sustainable advantage. Intel and AMD got into a chip productivity battle in the 1990s and spent billions but stayed basically even with each other. The phenomenon recalls the arms race between the US and the former Soviet Union, where both improved at a furious pace but neither could win—until the mid-1980s, when Reagan started seriously outspending the Soviets and pulled a big move on them.

Global toy and entertainment company Hasbro successfully achieved the top quintile of the Power Curve with a big move in productivity. Hasbro faced challenges managing a complex portfolio of businesses utilizing a large network of global outsourced vendors. Inefficiencies emerged through labor-intensive processes and communication lags across time zones, which became untenable when trends moved against the company—Hasbro's financial performance hit rock bottom with an operating loss of $104 million due to a big drop in toy revenue. Hasbro embarked on a turnaround, which aimed for it to be a smaller but more profitable version of itself with a focus on its core brands (for example, Transformers, Tonka, Play-Doh, and Monopoly).[5]

The following decade saw Hasbro consolidate business units and sites, invest in automated processing, invest in customer self-service, reduce headcount, and exit loss-making business units. Hasbro's SG&A expenses as a proportion of sales fell from an average of 42 percent at the beginning of the research period to 29 percent 10 years later. Sales productivity lifted, too—by a lot, in fact. Over the 10-year period, Hasbro shed more than a quarter of its workforce yet still grew total revenue by 33 percent (assisted by the successful launch of the *Transformers* movie franchise, an initiative led by current CEO Brian Goldner, who joined Hasbro in 2000 to take over the suffering US toys segment). Hasbro's total shareholder return grew at a CAGR of 15 percent over the decade.

German chemicals manufacturer BASF SE moved from the middle to the top of the Power Curve with the help of good endowment and positive trends, but it capitalized on this beneficial starting position with three big moves: programmatic M&A, resource re-allocation, and especially an improvement in both overhead and sales productivity. The moves helped lead to total shareholder return increasing at a CAGR of 17 percent over the decade.

BASF pays lots of attention to return on capital. When Chairman Jürgen Hambrecht took over in 2004, earning a "premium over our cost of capital" was the first point in his 10-year strategic plan. Achieving that meant making operations as efficient as possible and being prudent with the investment of new capital.

BASF saw productivity as a necessary way of "strengthening its competitiveness."[6] BASF's productivity improvements were particularly notable versus its peers in the chemicals industry. Over the decade, BASF successfully reduced its SG&A-to-sales ratio by 40 percent, while the median improvement in the industry was 25 percent. BASF lifted its sales productivity by 110 percent, versus the industry average improvement of 70 percent. Now, with an inside view, most managers would be thrilled with a 25 percent reduction in overhead and a 70 percent improvement in sales productivity—but with an outside view you see that's just keeping up; you have to do even better in the chemicals industry to make productivity a big move that creates competitive advantage.

How did BASF do it? The story has two main elements: merciless performance management with a focus on return on capital, and participation in the global trends of demand growth and industry consolidation.

BASF believes that its Verbund principle is instrumental in delivering world-class productivity. Verbund—literally "composite"—originates from BASF's flagship plants, which can manufacture a diverse range of finished products, thereby creating flexible capacity utilization and pooled use of inputs. BASF today has six such plants: two in Europe, two in North America, and two in Asia. But today, the Verbund concept permeates all of BASF, not just its production processes, which creates a culture of cooperation, knowledge-sharing, innovation, and operating efficiency throughout the organization. Verbund drives efficiency in the consumption of resources: capital, opex, and headcount.

Productivity matters, and it matters even more relative to other big moves when your business already is in the top quintile of companies on the Power Curve. Structuring and launching an effective, sustained productivity program is not easy, but in the age of machine learning and artificial intelligence, new tools to accelerate such programs are becoming mainstream. Previously unheard-of performance step changes, such as improving the productivity of R&D engineering teams by up to 30 percent over 24 months, are within reach now.[7]

Differentiation improvement

The fifth big move covers some of the more interesting aspects of strengthening the competitiveness of a business: innovation in products, services, and even business models. Differentiation improvement also covers gains in market share, such a common topic of conversation, and pricing, which—while admittedly not as sexy as innovation—is nonetheless a big lever for relative performance improvements.

Differentiation, expressed here in the comparison between the average gross margin of companies and that of their industry, is a way of summarizing just how much customers value a company's products and services relative to its competitors'. Based on our data set, we now know how much differentiation is required to make an impact: 30 percent. Your average gross margin needs to exceed your industry's by 30 percent over a decade for you to materially increase your chances of moving up the Power Curve.

German broadcaster ProSiebenSat.1 moved to the top quintile of the Power Curve by shifting its model for a new era of media with several innovations. One such strategy opened up ProSieben's addressable client base by using a "media for equity" offering for customers whose business would significantly benefit from mass media but who couldn't afford to pay with cash. Some of ProSieben's innovations were costly, sometimes even cannibalizing existing businesses. But, believing that the industry was going to move anyway, the company decided that experimenting with change was a matter of survival first and profitability second. ProSieben's gross margin expanded from 16 percent to 53 percent during our research period.

Memory card manufacturer SanDisk made a big move investing in innovation and ultimately improved its gross margins, leading to a 13 percent CAGR in total shareholder return over the decade.

Appreciating that it was a strong player in a good market, SanDisk went ahead of the industry in capital expenditure, reducing circuitry size, lowering manufacturing costs, and increasing output. SanDisk kept its prices at a premium to the market and invested heavily in trade promotion and its SanDisk Extreme Team, a public network of expert photographers, as a centerpiece of a lively and permanent social media presence. Over the 10 years, SanDisk successfully expanded its gross margins from 40 percent to 48 percent, while the broader industry experienced modest gross margin contraction. In the context of a good industry trend, SanDisk achieved average economic profit of $945 million at the end of the period, which moved it to the top quintile on the Power Curve.

At the beginning of our research period, British luxury fashion house Burberry was experiencing somewhat of an identity crisis, and its luxury status was under threat:

> By the early 2000s the company's distinctive camel-colored check had become the uniform of the "chav," the stereotypical white working-class delinquent looking for trouble. Bouncers and taxi drivers learned to turn away young men sporting Burberry baseball caps and jackets. . . . The brand's elite reputation seemed to be lost.[8]

The brand's defense against this apparent drift included vertical integration into the retail channel. Burberry grew its retail store footprint aggressively through Burberry-branded stores, concessions in department stores, and outlets. From having only 145 stores contributing 38 percent to group revenue in 2004, the company saw the retail channel grow to 497 stores plus digital commerce, contributing 70 percent of revenue a decade later.

The retail channel gave Burberry more control over the way customers interacted with its brand: Burberry now controls everything from the way sales staff greet customers and the training they receive, to the store ambiance and visual merchandising, to the consistency between stores and digital platforms and direct marketing. The stronger mix on retail gave gross margins a boost, by saving on the retailer's middleman margin, and increased bargaining power with its wholesale customers by reducing the brand's dependency on that channel. It's no fluke that, among retail companies on the Power Curve, those with vertically integrated models and premium brand positions (as well as those with fierce discount credentials) were much more likely to jump up quintiles than the traditional mid-market aggregator retail models.

Burberry also aspired to lead retail innovation with digital. Since 2006, with the appointment of CEO Angela Ahrendts, Burberry's vision has been to be "the first company that is fully digital." Social media is now crucial to the brand's relationship with modern consumers, and the company's followers exceed 40 million across many platforms. Burberry aims to provide seamless interaction between the brand's physical and digital presences. For example, the flagship store on Regent Street in London has interactive digital mirrors that respond to RFID chips embedded in products. Point of sale has moved from the checkout to the sofa, where shoppers can use digital payment technologies such as Apple Pay. Burberry runway shows are live-streamed in 3D, and store launches have become avant-garde digital showcases; at the 2014 launch of Burberry's Shanghai store, a partnership with WeChat allowed subscribers to immerse themselves in 360 degrees of fashion, music, and dance. This, of course, is also a brilliant example of strategic capital re-allocation.

Furthermore, Burberry leveraged the brand into adjacent product lines. In 2004, accessories and children's contributed only 30 percent of group revenue. By 2014, these categories grew to 40 percent of group sales revenue. Burberry also successfully launched a high-margin beauty products range, which grew to 7 percent of group revenue.

With a greater mix of retail and new higher-margin product lines, as well as investment in supply chain to meet digital needs and keep supply costs low, Burberry's gross margin expanded from 59 percent at the beginning of our research to 76 percent at the end. Economic profit rose from $92 million to $435 million, putting it deservedly in the top quintile of the Power Curve. Total shareholder return grew at a CAGR of 17 percent over the decade.

Much of what goes into differentiation is hard to do. It's difficult to find all the niches where you can stand out. Innovation befuddles many. Even if they can spot trends in technology that could benefit them, for example, bringing those inside the business is more easily aspired to than done.

Differentiation requires long-term thinking—which is hard while you're on the quarterly earnings treadmill. Have we not cut the R&D budget when we needed to make this year's budget? A fascinating analysis on the impact of private ownership shows that private firms invest approximately double the rate that similar matched public firms do. Engaging in the quarterly earnings game really does drive short-termism.[9] Did we not launch a product prematurely, sacrificing some margin, to make sure we had good news for the market? There is hardly an area in the repertoire of strategic moves that is more easily sacrificed for short-term gain than the differentiation lever.

"I HAD A LONG TERM PLAN BUT
I CAN'T REMEMBER WHAT IT WAS."

Are you playing to your advantage?

This is where management objectives, incentives, and the long-term interest of shareholders often collide. When we use the 10 Timeless Tests of Strategy[10] to check the quality of strategies, it is often Test #2 that leads to the most extensive and revealing discussions: "Does your strategy tap your true source of competitive advantage?" In other words: "Does it strengthen your differentiation?"

That breaks into two questions.

First, do you understand what the source of your competitive advantage is? Do you know why you make money today? These turn out to be incredibly interesting questions. If you ask 10 people, you get as many different answers.

At a retail bank in Australia, for instance, the leaders wanted to expand into overseas markets. The logic was: We're very successful, so we must be better operators than our competitors. We'll move into other markets, where the operations aren't nearly as efficient as in our home markets, and we'll clean up. When we looked at how the bank actually made money, though, all the operating metrics were unimpressive. They made money based on product strategy: They had a big exposure to residential mortgages, for which demand was very strong in Australia at the time. The even bigger source of profit was that the bank was superb at picking branch locations. But the choices were made by two guys in a back office, so there wasn't any reason to suspect that they would be anywhere near as successful in Indonesia or other new countries.

Second, do you leverage what makes you special?

When we looked into why multi-business conglomerates in Asia grew successfully, we found a very different strategy. On average, they entered a new business every 18 months. Almost 70 percent of their moves were driven by M&A, and half of the growth came from step-out moves, not acquisitions in adjacent markets or in their value chains. That seemed odd. But further investigation found that each acquisition leveraged an important capability, even if that wasn't immediately obvious. It wasn't just that a company knew an industry; it might be that someone had a special relationship. They were in online gaming and knew the regulators, so they expanded into banking. They were in real estate, so they had land, and they moved into large-scale manufacturing. While the strategies might have looked unusual, there were smart people at the helm of these companies, and they very much understood both how they made money and how they could turn those competitive advantages into more money.

Big moves make for good strategy

Understanding the role of big moves in your strategy is more than just what they are and how they work in isolation, it's also how they work together. The following dynamics are the most important to understand about big moves—and about the very fabric of good strategy.

Big moves are really valuable. The beauty of empirics is that we now know how much your big moves add to the value of a company. Check out the matrix in Exhibit 28. It shows the expected economic

Exhibit 28

The value of moves vs inheritance
Inheritance and moves both matter!

Expected 2010–14 economic profit for firms starting in the middle 3 quintiles
$ Millions

		Inheritance (Endowment and Trend together)		
		Poor inheritance	Neutral inheritance	Strong inheritance
Moves	Strong moves	260	1,069	1,360
	Neutral moves	(22)	182	1,102
	Poor moves	(70)	2	161

Source: McKinsey Corporate Performance Analytics™

profit in 2010–14 of a firm starting in the middle-tier in 2000–4, based on the endowment and trend they inherit (the columns) and the strengths of their moves (the rows).

Two things stand out. First, cast your eyes north-south, and you see—no matter what the inheritance—it always pays to add more big moves. Second, look down the diagonal. What you will see is that roughly speaking, really big moves can "cancel out" the impact of a poor inheritance. In other words, strong moves with a poor inheritance ($260 million) is about as valuable as poor moves with a strong inheritance ($161 million). Of course, if you could choose you would have both and get a whopping expected payoff of $1.36 billion—but only a handful of firms manage to do that.

Even small improvements in odds have a dramatic impact on the expected payoff, owing to the extremely steep rise of the Power Curve.

For example, the probability-weighted expected value of middle-tier companies increasing their odds to 27 percent from the average of 8 percent is $123 million—nearly three times the total average economic profit for middle-tier companies.

Big moves are non-linear. Many business leaders would lean back and say, "Of course, these five moves are part of our strategy." But that's not true. Even for many businesses that have these levers articulated in their strategies, the businesses are not executing on the moves—at least not enough to make a real difference.

As we've shown, making modest efforts on these five moves doesn't improve your odds. Moves are non-linear. Just pulling a lever does not help. You need to pull it hard enough to make a difference. For instance, as we've noted, productivity improvements that are roughly in line with the improvement rates of the industry you are playing in do not matter. The probability of moving up only improves above a certain threshold—in the case of productivity improvements, for instance, your rate needs to be at least 25 percent above the industry average to make a difference. You are only making a big move if you have cleared the threshold for its respective lever.

Big moves must be big relative to your industry. Even if you're improving on all five measures, what matters is how you stack up against your competitors. You need to outrun if you want to win. Locked inside the stuffy strategy room, amid the detailed introspection, teams can lose sight of the fact that they aren't the only ones in the industry. Chances are, their competitors are working hard, too. Managers may still think they're being aggressive with their moves, and they might have grand plans about how high their margins can get and who they're going to take over, but the reality is that everyone is trying to do the same thing. If everybody cuts costs by 5 percent or brings out a similar product, where's the advantage? You have to do the work, but that's just keeping up.

Big moves compound. One move isn't enough, either, if you really want to improve your odds. Moves are additive. Making one move is good, two is much better, and three is much better than that. Without getting deep into the math, the basic idea is that making one move will nearly double your odds of making it from the middle quintiles to the top. A second move roughly doubles those odds again. A third nearly doubles the odds again, and so on. That math isn't exactly accurate, but it illustrates how two or three moves could take you from your initial odds—8 percent—and give you a better-than-even chance of reaching the top quintile—even only with average scores on endowment and trends. While even one move is hard, in the face of the pressure from the social side of strategy, it's important to pull as many levers as you can.

Big moves are asymmetric. Here's the good news: Four of the five moves are asymmetric. In other words, the upside possibility far outweighs the downside risk. While M&A is often touted as high-risk, when it comes to whether you move up or down the Power Curve, organic strategies are just as risky, and programmatic M&A not only increases your odds of moving up the curve but simultaneously decreases your odds of sliding down. These are truly one-sided bets. The same is true for improving your productivity or gross margin relative to your industry. Making those moves increases your odds of winning while decreasing your risks. Resource re-allocation slightly increases the chances of moving down, because you may be moving into an industry with a poorer trend than your current industry, but nearly doubles the odds of reaching the top quintile. Capex is the only lever that symmetrically changes the odds of going up and down. By increasing capex, your chances of going up on the Power Curve increase, but so do the chances of dropping down. A big capex play amplifies rather than tilts the odds, reinforcing the importance of choosing very carefully the industry and geographic trends you are betting on.

The fear among executives is that making big moves might improve the odds of moving up but might also bring more risk of stumbling—but that narrative is false. We can now prove that pulling these five levers improves the odds of going up the Power Curve and reduces the odds of going down.

There goes the excuse for "playing it safe," for having low ambition, or for not pushing the organization to outperform at least your own industry.

In fact, not moving is probably the riskiest strategy of all. You not only risk stagnation on the Power Curve but you miss out on an additional reward that is completely inaccessible to non-movers: growth capital. It mostly flows to the winners, condemning many laggards to playing along.

Big moves are cumulative, not silver bullets. You don't just wake up one day and decide you're going to have better productivity and then expect it to be there the next day. Rather, what you'll find is that making these big moves is really the accumulation of good practices that build up over time. The companies that successfully deliver on their big moves make them a part of their day-to-day mantra. It's the constancy of purpose that makes moves turn into big moves.

• • •

When you think about it, the analysis of endowment, trends, and moves is a rather new way of looking at good strategy and what it takes to execute strategy in the real-life context of our companies. We have measured the probability of good strategy, explained how you can know your own odds, and explored the levers that you need to pull to improve your odds and get to big moves.

We now have the "outside view" that can be used to address the social side of strategy. With this, there is hope that good strategy is possible—for you and for your business.

In the next and final chapter, we will get very practical about what you can do to improve your chances of beating the odds.

Chapter 8

Eight shifts to unlock strategy

Let's get very practical: There is a new way to give your strategy a chance, and it's going to take eight big shifts.

We started this journey of discovery by wondering how it could be that, in today's world of big data analytics, the hockey stick remains the iconic image of strategy even though so few pan out. We were puzzled that challenges, such as peanut buttering that were talked and written about 40 or 50 years ago remain so similar to the challenges that business leaders share with us all the time. They wish to re-allocate resources to more attractive growth opportunities, for instance, but still find that resources are as sticky as glue.

After reading the previous chapters, you might agree that we are at the brink of a very different—and much more exciting—era in strategy. We now know the odds of strategy; we now know what we can do to improve those odds; and we can now much better define strategies, i.e., the big moves that beat the odds.

One hurdle remains: While we better understand how the social side of strategy prevents big moves, we still haven't fully prescribed how to effectively address these social barriers. The question remaining, the one we want to try to answer in this final chapter, is the one that probably matters most to you: What does all this mean for how you run your strategy process, how you lead your team, how you create and execute strategies, and how you can achieve better business outcomes?

Honoring our pledge to not throw new frameworks at you, we still want to offer reflections about how to change your game in very practical ways that will help you break through the social barriers. We will propose eight shifts, specific areas where you can change what's happening in your strategy room—practical shifts that you can work on starting Monday morning.

The eight shifts synthesize what we have learned about how to address the social side of strategy (see Exhibit 29).

Exhibit 29

Eight shifts in a nutshell

1.	from	Annual Planning	to Strategy as a Journey
2.	from	Getting to "Yes"	to Debating Real Alternatives
3.	from	Peanut Butter	to Picking your 1-in-10s
4.	from	Approving Budgets	to Making Big Moves
5.	from	Budget Inertia	to Liquid Resources
6.	from	Sandbagging	to Open Risk Portfolios
7.	from	You Are Your Numbers	to Holistic Perspective on Performance
8.	from	Long-Range Planning	to Forcing the First Step

1. From annual planning . . . to strategy as a journey

When you ask business leaders around the world where they make most strategy decisions, the answer is rarely "in the strategy room or the boardroom." You are much more likely to hear: "in the shower before I went to meet my senior team," or "over that dinner conversation with the CEO of my major customer." One of our clients in East Asia regularly makes the most important business decisions on the golf course in consultation with his three fortune tellers, with whom he regularly plays (we are not kidding). Others confirm that "going for a walk with other key decision makers" helps them with alignment and direction setting and reduces anxiety and opposition.

What's broken in the strategy room?

As important as a regular planning cycle might be for ensuring that all important questions are being surfaced and that budget processes are being informed, a regular, standardized cycle is not terribly well suited to the dynamic nature of today's business environment.[1]

In fact, trying to solve your big strategic questions and lock down an agreed plan at the same time can be near impossible. You can be sure the urgent will dominate the important, and those big questions won't get the air-time. Besides, those messy non-linear and uncertain strategic issues don't fit into the linear world of the 3- to 5-year plan.

Even if the dynamics in the strategy room were perfect, the world doesn't unfold in nice, neat, annual increments. Things change all the time, both in your business and in the markets around you. Potential deals do not occur when you have your annual board strategy session; they occur when they occur, and you need to be ready. Why not discuss some of the key strategic questions and performance every week, or month, at a minimum, complementing traditional annual strategic planning processes?

STRATEGY AS A JOURNEY

- Hold regular strategy dialogues instead of just an annual process
- Track your portfolio of initiatives across multiple horizons and update your strategy based on progress
- Monitor a 3-years-back/3-years-forward rolling plan—if you want to track numbers

Hold regular strategy dialogues. Say you trimmed your annual process to the bare minimum—we can almost hear many of you and your managers sighing with relief. Instead, you launch more regular, incisive strategy conversations with your team—perhaps as a fixed space on your monthly management team meeting. You start maintaining a "live" list of the most important strategic issues, a list of your big moves, and a pipeline of initiatives for executing them.

You would get a lot closer to achieving continuous engagement on strategy. Every time you meet as a team, you update each other quickly on the state of the market and your business, then reflect on your issues, big moves, and initiatives. You consider whether they remain appropriate, should be modified, or should be stopped. Every time you meet, you also do a deep dive into one or a few topics of opportunity or concern.

Track your portfolio of initiatives. Your strategy will evolve like a pipeline of initiatives working through different stage-gates.[2] Long-dated and prospective ideas will be like "real options" where the critical path is about learning and achieving familiarity. For initiatives that are about scaling growth in a 3-year horizon, the emphasis will be on managing capital investments, achieving milestones, and showing strong user acceptance. For initiatives that are short-term and in highly familiar territory, you will be looking at in-year financial delivery. The pipeline should have movement in it, too—it's designed to flow over time rather than be a "set and forget" plan.

Your team will never need to write again a 150-page deck that is the basis for so much social gaming and manipulation. You won't need to wait a year to see that that hockey stick was just going to be another hair on the back. People will know that they will be continually accountable, so they will be less likely to sandbag or make bold claims in a bid for resources—even if they do continue the traditional behavior, the offenses will become apparent a lot sooner and will be easier to catch.

Those false hockey sticks will mostly go away. They happen because of the disconnected dynamic between the 5-year strategy and the 1-year operating plan, but those now become rolling plans. Because you are constantly staying on top of what is happening and why around your big moves, you will have a much better sense for what is truly causing success and failure. No more "success is because of manage-ment excellence" and "failure is due to one-off, external events."

Monitor a rolling plan. This continuous approach leaves the question of how you get to a plan and a budget from these monthly conversations. You may continue a bare-bones annual process, but, more likely, you will move to a rolling, 12-month plan that you update as needed. You might also have a 2- to 10-year plan on stage all the time in the strategy sessions that you adjust if you change initiatives, priorities, and big moves. Every big move leads to an update of the expected trajectory of the business. You are moving all the time—just like the world around you.

The strategy process will be less formulaic and more adapted to the needs of businesses at any given point. It will be a journey of almost continuous checks of whether the assumptions made in a strategy still hold, whether the strategy needs a refresh, or whether the context has moved so much that new strategies are required. The *strategy process will be a journey* that meanders dynamically through the corporation, help-ing to navigate highly competitive industries and fast-moving trends.

Tencent, for one, has a highly adaptable strategy process that can react immediately to changes in the marketplace. They're making, in some years, hundreds of acquisitions, so they're constantly adapting and changing and moving based on new information. Tencent has a broad strategic direction toward developing their platform and new elements of the platform, but the fundamentals—the big moves—change as a result of a continuing dialogue among the management team and in reaction to changes in their business context.

2. From getting to "yes" . . . to debating real alternatives

Most planning discussions bring one plan into the room. Success is seen as approving that singular plan. Then we can all go home and be happy. The most annoying thing that can happen, then, is for some-one to question the premise of the plan, or to open up the solution space and bring different options into the room. But of course, we all know that this deeper reflection is exactly what is needed to get to real strategies.

Think of it this way: Real strategy is about making your hard-to-reverse choices about how to win. Planning is about how to make those choices happen. But the first step is being skipped too often, even if we try to make ourselves feel okay by labeling the plan "strategic." There's simply no point in precisely planning for the wrong future.

DISCUSSING REAL ALTERNATIVES

- Frame strategy around "hard to reverse" choices
- Calibrate aspirations against your endowment, trends, and moves to bring an "outside view" into the room
- Compare real alternative plans with different risk and investment profiles
- Track assumptions over time, and build contingencies into your plans so you can evolve your choices as you learn more
- Use de-biasing techniques to ensure quality decision making

---

Frame strategy as choices. What if your strategy decisions looked like this picture in Exhibit 30? This would be very different than signing off on another plan. By reframing the strategy discussion as a choice-making rather than a plan-making exercise, the whole conversation will change.

To build your own strategy decision grid, identify the major axes of choice—they have to be "hard to reverse" choices. Think of them as the things the next management team will have to take as a given. Then, for each choice dimension, describe three to five possible but different choices. The overall strategic options will be the few coherent bundles of these choices. Focus your debate—and your analysis—on the few most difficult choices.

Calibrate your strategy. What if every strategy document had a version of the analysis of endowment, trends, and moves that we've laid out and included an "odds score," describing the chances of moving up the Power Curve? Now, wouldn't that reframe the conversations? You won't just run through the decks and be led to a "yes." You'd see that many traditional approaches to strategy won't work. You'd have to go back to square one and try again. You'd have to consider real alternatives that likely lead you to bigger moves than you've made in the past.

Exhibit 30

Sample decision grids for food retailers
True strategy gets to the hard-to-reverse big choices

Strategic decisions	Alternatives			TESCO
Price position	Lowest possible	Soft discount	**Mainstream**	Premium
Range	1,200 SKUs	12,500 SKUs	**40,000 SKUs**	
Brands	>90% Private	**~50% Private**	Brand led	
Loyalty	None	**Loyalty cards**		
Network	Smaller, cheaper	Smaller, prime	**Larger**	
Service level	Bare bones	**Moderate**	High touch	
Category mix	Core + one-offs	Focus on food	**Extended range**	

Strategic decisions	Alternatives			ALDI
Price position	**Lowest possible**	Soft discount	Mainstream	Premium
Range	**1,200 SKUs**	12,500 SKUs	40,000 SKUs	
Brands	**>90% Private**	~50% Private	Brand led	
Loyalty	**None**	Loyalty cards		
Network	**Smaller, cheaper**	Smaller, prime	Larger	
Service level	**Bare bones**	Moderate	High touch	
Category mix	**Core + one-offs**	Focus on food	Extended range	

In a world where we are just focused on getting to "yes," plans can end up being discussed in a vortex, with no reliable calibration. Now, based on what we've explained about the empirics of strategy, you can test a strategy with real facts. Explicitly using the "outside view" about your aspirations and big moves can help you overcome some of the biases that let the social side bog down the discussions in the strategy room. You get the opportunity to move away from those 150-page decks that are designed to create diversions and numb the audience into saying "yes" to the proposal.

Even staying put on the Power Curve is often a lot of hard work, and most management teams and their leaders don't want to just stay put. They want to push the envelope, to stretch themselves. The problem is that "hard work" and "pushing the envelope" have very little to do with the real issue: moving on the Power Curve.

Moves on the Power Curve are *relative to competition*—and, guess what, your competitors are pushing the envelope, too. Of course they are! We often hear teams complain about their CEOs overloading them with initiatives. The question is: Which are the right big moves that can realistically get you ahead of your competition? Those initiatives should get all your attention, should absorb all your efforts. Remember that boardroom across town, where your competitor is discussing how they are going to grow their market share just like you are.

When Bill Gates was CEO of Microsoft in the 1990s, he spent as much as half of product review sessions interrogating developers about what they were hearing about competing products and about what, theoretically, others could do that would get in the way of Microsoft's plans. That focus on the competition certainly worked for him, and it can work for you.

Compare alternative plans. We can already hear you thinking, "Great—more data. Isn't that just an invitation for the next game of getting to a yes?" Maybe. But you can try to avoid the problem by forcing a discussion around strategic alternatives that management believes to be at similar risk/return levels, instead of a single big move. Then force the discussion on which big move to make. Or, show different plan scenarios with different levels of resourcing and risk so you can make real, quantified trade-offs rather than being forced to make "all or nothing choices."

Track assumptions over time. A few short weeks after the plan is developed, the detailed assumptions go into a fog of memory. The variance to budget gets tracked very carefully, but the underlying assumptions—such as uptake rates, market growth, and inflation rates—are not tracked as carefully. Imagine if there was an "assumptions budget" that was tracked as carefully as the financial budget?

Come approval time, we love concrete plans, but as the real world plays out, with all its uncertainty, we come to hate the rigidity. Let's stop planning as though we know the future. Rather, decide what you can today, with the information you have, and build explicit trigger points into the strategy to make better decisions as you learn more. Running strategy as a journey (shift one) will enable this.

De-bias decision making. Warren Buffett is said to operate with red and blue teams, even at times hiring two investment banking teams to evaluate a possible acquisition. One argues in favor, the other against. Both are offered success fees, payable only if Buffett decides that their argument wins. Private equity firms have found that more than 30 percent of decisions are different when opposing possibilities are pitted against each other. That is a big deal!

There are, of course, many other great de-biasing techniques. One we regularly use is a "pre mortem," where you assume a strategy has failed to achieve its intended objective after, say, 2 years.[3] Then, you brainstorm as a team what caused the failure, and how it might have been avoided. This safely gets many big issues out on the table.

This is where your qualities as a business leader can have tremendous impact on the trajectory of your company. Give yourself a break. End the nauseatingly boring and paralyzing pseudo-strategy discussions that, in reality, are purely about getting to "yes." Instead, give your team and yourself a chance to debate your real choices.

3. From peanut butter . . . to picking your 1-in-10s

Peanut butter is the biggest enemy of big moves. It is near impossible to make big moves if resources are peanut buttered across all businesses and operations. Our data show that you're far more likely to make a major move up the Power Curve because one or two businesses let you break out, rather than because every business or operation improved in lockstep.

To move, you have to identify the break-out opportunities as early as possible and feed them all the resources they need. That means getting your team to align behind the likely winners—and that's where the problem usually starts. Despite the best intentions, peanut butter seeps back into the process.

Intellectually, it's actually easier than you might think to identify the likely winners in your portfolio. If you were to ask your management team to identify the most likely winners in the portfolio, they will probably strongly agree on #1 and maybe #2—much less so on, say, what ranks #7 or #8. We have done exercises with dozens of management teams and rarely found that "picking your 1-in-10s" is hard. That's really not the issue. The problems start when the discussion moves to resource allocation—because that's where the social side of strategy kicks in.

Some industries seem to intuitively grasp that you have to kiss a lot of frogs before you find the prince. In fashion, people understand that the one hit out of 10 is what matters. The same is true in movies, oil exploration, venture capital, and some others. But most other businesses do not have a "hit mentality," or, in other words, they lack appreciation for probabilities.

PICKING YOUR 1-IN-10S

- Adjust incentives so the team supports the resource re-allocation
- Pick where to compete on a granular level, maybe even by vote
- Allocate resources from a portfolio-level view and skew toward opportunity
- Play to win—allocate enough resources to outcompete others in the key areas

Adjust incentives to encourage resource re-allocation. To move away from peanut buttering resources, you will need to explicitly address the motivation of the team and structure both performance management and incentives accordingly. If some people are taking a bullet for the team, they need to know why and what's in it for them. In our experience, it does take considerable leadership to get everyone to line up behind skewing resource allocations, but just having the conversation about the 1-in-10 starts to reset expectations and change the nature of the dialogue.

Pick where to compete at a granular level. One thing that really gets in the way of dynamic resource re-allocation is excessive aggregation and averaging. You can't see the true variance of opportunity when things get rolled up into big profit centers. Instead, develop more granular opportunity maps—with at least 30 to 100 cells—then decide where to move resources.

By the way, this 1-in-10 idea is a sort of fractal. It applies at every level of a company, where managers should identify their most likely candidates to break out and should pour resources into them.

We've seen many senior teams move away from peanut buttering by using some form of voting to pick priorities. In some cases, that's a secret ballot in envelopes. In other cases, CEOs set up a grand matrix showing all the opportunity cells and let executives allocate points to various initiatives by applying stickers to the matrix. Whatever the approach, we find that, most of the time, there is strong agreement on what the very best opportunities are. The same holds true, by the way, for agreeing on what the likely duds are. Not hard at all. It's the broad middle where views diverge and resources get squandered.

Allocate resources at a portfolio level. Just because you are organized one way doesn't mean that is the only way you should look at the market. In fact, if resources are allocated in too much of a "trickle down" fashion as they move down the company hierarchy, you will never get the radical kind of resource shift you need. Studies have shown that resource allocation decisions change a lot when a company's structure shifts—even though nothing else has changed.[4]

One of us recently completed a study for a client where instead of rolling up plans at a business unit level, we went one level down. We built the detailed curve of the 60 or so specific investible opportunities they had, irrespective of which business they came from. The result? A much bigger shift in resources to the best opportunities that tended to get "averaged out" in a more democratic process.

We've also seen how founder-owners often keep all major decisions to themselves. There's no incentive, then, to peanut butter resources. They often survey executives to get input on where to invest but make the decisions on their own. They are much nimbler in deploying resources decisively to the most promising initiatives. We view them as exemplary for how business leaders should go about finishing off the peanut butter business.

Play to win. Now that you have a granular view, and are making resource allocation decisions at a portfolio level, the next step is to truly distort resources so you can win. Don't just look at the resources relative to your other opportunities: Remember that big moves have to be big versus the world, so you have to base your decisions on what the best competitors are doing. That may mean radical change.

4. From approving budgets . . . to making big moves

We've discussed how the social side of strategy can make the 3-year plan a cover for the real game: negotiating year 1, which becomes the budget. Managers tend to be interested in years 2 and 3 but absolutely fascinated by year 1, because that is where they live and die. So, we need a shift to end the situation where the strategy is little more than the opening act to the budget.

One of the worst culprits in these budget-driven discussions is the "base case"—some version of a planned business case, anchored in a number of (largely opaque) assumptions about the context and the company strategy. The base case is rarely anchored in a firm understanding of actual business performance. It's more like a drift anchor, a reference point that floats among context and assumptions, with last year being the only real reference point. The base case is the manifestation of the inside view in the strategy discussion. Why is that a problem? Well, for one, the base case may obscure the view of where the business actually stands, which makes it hard to see what realistic aspirations should be, and certainly what strategic moves could deliver on those aspirations.

Many budgets and plans we see have gaps in them, portions of the projection that don't have a rationale attached to them. These gaps are often classified as "business as usual," things managers promise to deliver as part of leading their organizations. The managers request resources for operating expenses and people that can only be justified by closing these gaps, but it's largely unclear how that's supposed to happen—and the actions executed under "business as usual" typically do nothing to help a unit or the whole business make big moves.

Aren't discussions about targets a drag? Imagine if you could turn these discussions on their head. What if, instead of forcing decisions on targets and making uncertain promises, you could focus the strategy dialogue on big moves, on your best ideas for how to beat the market? Then just let the outcomes follow.[5]

MAKING BIG MOVES

- Build a "momentum case" instead of a base case
- Do a "tear down" of past results to see what came from trends and what came from moves
- "Mind the gap": Check that the plan is big enough to fill the gap between the momentum line and the aspiration
- Benchmark the big moves relative to competition to test that they are big enough to really move the needle
- Separate the discussion on moves from the discussion on budgets: One should follow the other

---

Build a momentum case. A practical way to avoid this trap is to forget the base case. Instead, although this can be a bit awkward, challenge yourself and the people working on your strategy to build a proper "momentum case." This is a simple version of the future that presumes that the trajectory of a business's current performance is going to continue as it has over the preceding period. The momentum case discards presumptions about new and miraculous market share gains and ignores all claims of productivity improvements. The momentum case essentially strips down the business plan to its bare minimum of just continuing the current business momentum—the highly probable trajectory without any additional actions.

Anchoring in the momentum case will already help you avoid the first causes of unrealistic hockey sticks and hairy backs. You'll have a better sense of how far you really need to go, rather than just assuming the progress that invariably shows up in the base case. You'll see how much impact your big moves need to deliver to change the trajectory of the business. Without a well-documented momentum case, it's hard to sort fact from fiction in your strategy discussion.

Do a "tear-down" of your results. Even with the momentum case, you still have to absolutely understand and be explicit about why your business is making money today. That knowledge lets you take the bias out of decisions about what risks to take and about managerial performance and rewards. Not being clear about what actually drives performance lets the social side of strategy rear its ugly head and causes many flawed strategies. Think about the BU head who managed to bring the business to break-even in a very tough competitive context, vs. the BU head who generates huge profits in a virtually monopolistic situation. Who will be better rewarded in most incentive discussions? And how will that affect the way people think about strategy and behave in the strategy room?

It's actually not that hard to perform a tear-down—the momentum case is typically a much tougher exercise. In a tear-down, you just take the business's past performance and build a "bridge"—that is, isolate the different contributions that explain the changes in performance. This is something most CFOs do regularly for factors like forex changes and inflation. The "bridge" needs to consider average industry performance and growth, the impact of sub-market selection, and the effect of M&A.

Mind the gap. Now that you have a thorough, unbiased understanding of where your business stands and what drives performance, you can calibrate your aspirations. Then, most importantly, you can size up just how big your moves need to be to close the gap between the momentum case and the aspiration. You will see the full size of the task ahead, not assuming some stuff as "business as usual" but tallying up all the work the enterprise needs to do to diverge from the momentum case. Nothing wrong with a big gap between momentum and aspiration if you have the big moves to fill it up.

Let's upend this disappointing dynamic about targets in the strategy room: Don't just ask for a target or a budget. Also ask for the 20 things each of your business leaders wants to do to produce a series of big moves over the coming period. Then debate the big moves, rather than the numbers that are supposed to result from these moves.

Why should we do this big move? Why shouldn't we? How does the company look different depending on what risk and resource threshold we set for the big moves?

A shift in focus on moves will also bring into the strategy room some discussions that, as we've shown, are very important but that don't often make it into the conversation. M&A is one of the big moves you can make, but it's often treated on a separate track. Productivity and differentiation, two of the other five big moves, are typically treated as part of an operational performance review even though, as we've seen, they're strategic differentiators. M&A, productivity, and differentiation all need to be discussed explicitly as part of strategy discussions, not in terms of numerical targets but in terms of how you can turn them into big moves, into gaining advantage over your competitors.

Benchmark the moves. Instead of the standard, 150-page set of details, ask each manager for a set of big moves, calibrated against what the competition has been doing and is expected to do. If a business leader requests additional resources, you approve them based on whether or not you believe the big moves she is proposing could lead to a real hockey stick and whether you trust her to pull them off. If the plan does not include big moves, then targets and resources get lowered. Budgets are not tied to targets; budgets are tied to big moves.

Talk about moves first, budgets second. This focus on big moves will get away from the incrementalism that comes with the normal process—"Last year, we did X, so this year we can probably do X plus a little." You also get away from the risk aversion that comes with the normal process, which treats every issue at the same time. With this shift, the big moves come first. The consideration of risks, while obviously important, comes later.

Everybody will know that, if they do not have big moves and cannot instill confidence about pulling off big moves, they will lose resources accordingly.

Here is your chance to cut through the social side of strategy and dispense once and for all with the largely fact-free advice written in most business books about strategy. If you want to put strategy back into the strategy room, just evolve the strategy dialogue around big moves—based on facts, calibrated against competition, and informed by your experience and judgment.

5. From budget inertia . . . to liquid resources

Let's assume decisions are made all around big moves. How do we avoid an unpleasant awakening? Let's say it's budget time in late October, and we want to make a big move, allocating 15 percent of all capex and opex across our businesses to new growth opportunities. But . . . oops . . . nothing happens. Why? Well, we don't have the resources. We can't just pull out 10–20 percent of the opex budget of a fully running business without warning. Nobody could do that responsibly.

To mobilize resources and budgets, there needs to be a certain level of resource liquidity. Most businesses do not create resource liquidity upfront, but resource liquidity is, in essence, the currency of strategy. How can you make a strategic bet if you don't have any resources to put on the table?

We believe that the handover between strategy and execution happens when the resources are made available to follow through on big moves. Execution can then begin, and managers can be held accountable. They no longer have the excuse of resource constraints.

LIQUID RESOURCES

- Start freeing up resources as much as a year before your strategy will need to deploy them
- Move to "80 percent–based budgeting" to unlock a kitty of contestable resources
- Charge managers an opportunity cost for their resources, so they have an incentive to free them up

---

Free up resources beforehand. You need to get started early—on January 1, or whenever your fiscal year begins. That's when serious productivity improvement initiatives need to be under way to free resources by the time resource allocations will be decided later in the year. Resources can be freed in many other ways, too, through divestitures, capital injections, etc. The reason why we highlight productivity is that strategic resources are not just about cash. Opex and talent are often equal, if not more important, resources that need to be freed to be re-allocated.

Then you need determination. If you want resources to be available to be re-allocated, you need to hold on to them after they have been freed. If there were physical laws in business, one of the strongest would be that all resources dissipate instantly. Your R&D organization will have the most creative new product ideas as soon as an engineer has time; a sales force will identify the most attractive new business opportunities as soon as the productivity program has freed a part of the sales force. Being incredibly clear about separating the initiatives that free resources from the opportunities to re-invest them is foundational to any meaningful productivity gain—and for holding on to resources that you intend to re-allocate.

Make an "80 percent–based" budget. You might have heard of "zero-based budgets"—the idea that every single dollar should be put in the docks and earned on merits. It's a nice idea, and will make a lot of sense in specific times and situations. But you can't run an operation one year at a time, and you can't hire and fire an entire workforce every year. What you can do is force a certain sliver of the budget to be contestable every year. Here we say 20 percent, just as a marker—in some cases, 10 percent might be more realistic. The point is to force money back into the pot every year, freeing it for re-allocation. Remember: To re-allocate, you need to de-allocate.

A related idea is to set high targets for improvement—which are distinct from growth goals—to generate a continual kitty of resources. Rather than just delivering their numbers, leaders in a business are tasked with freeing up a certain percentage of resources via productivity on the base business *as well as* continually delivering on new growth initiatives.

Place an opportunity cost on resources. One common problem is that resources can be thought of as "free" if they don't directly hit your specific budget. For example, in many retailers, the category managers are tasked with driving sales and gross margins in their categories. Yet the scarce resources needed to deliver those gains—the limited shelf space and costly inventory—are often not measured as hard. As a result, category managers don't want to give up space or cut back on inventory, even though doing so would free up resources for other opportunities. In the retail case, the answer is pretty simple: Use ratios. If the category manager is measured on sales per square foot (return on space) and stock turns (return on inventory), then the incentives to release resources to more productive uses are stronger. In other cases, the solutions may be more complex but, nonetheless, need to be found to make sure that resources are allocated as effectively as possible.

Without continual freeing of resources, strategy becomes a paper exercise constrained by a limited budget. That doesn't work in a world where big moves are required. As you create resource liquidity, you breathe fresh air into the strategy room. Big moves become possible.

NXP had 14 businesses when they spun off from Philips. Over time, NXP moved all its resources to 2 businesses and freed cash and people from all the others. These 1-in-10 choices in automotive and identification, backed by full resource shifts, were big moves that created a winning streak for NXP—the likely movers were "resourced to win."

6. From sandbagging . . . to open risk portfolios

When BUs develop strategic plans, as we all know, they sandbag their targets. As you aggregate these plans on a corporate level, the buffers add up to a corporate sandbag that makes the hairy back virtually a certainty. Because of risk avoidance, you don't have goals set and resources allocated in ways that allow for a break-out performance. The mechanism of aggregating BU strategies also explains why we see so few big moves proposed at the corporate level: Many M&A initiatives and other bold programs are simply viewed as too risky by individual BU heads. These initiatives never make the final list that they bring into the strategy room.

Sandbagging is, we admit, a complex problem that is hard to untangle. Let's say a leadership team of a business unit plans for margin improvement, perhaps 10 percent of sales. The leader doesn't want to overcommit, so he corrects for risk and promises only to deliver 5 points. Then he thinks, if I have 5 points "free" I will invest in good growth ideas. He winds up with a lot of flexibility—a sandbag. If margin does not improve, he has his risk buffer. But he may give up on the attempt to pursue margin improvement beyond the 5 points he's promised. He also may be taking on considerable risk to invest in growth, the effects of which will only be noticed later.

"Are we sure the target is big enough?"

But we have also seen teams make strides against sandbagging. The fundamental idea is to move away from the current dynamic of "sandbag the budget, hockey stick the strategy" to a situation where risks and investments are managed on an aggregate level. Put differently, the idea is to move from aggregating lots of individual budget sandbags together from the bottom up and to creating a single, corporate-level view. Move from hockey sticks everywhere to one corporate-level hockey stick that's based on a series of plausible big moves. We all naturally tend toward sandbagging because, after all, everyone does it—but grouping the discussion of risk tosses out that rationale.

OPEN RISK PORTFOLIOS

- Force separate conversations for improvement, growth, and risk
- Make risk versus growth decisions at a portfolio level, not within BUs
- Tailor approaches on "no-regret moves," "big bets," and "real options"
- Adjust incentives and measures to reflect the risk people are taking

Force separate conversations. You can move from one integrated strategy review to three sequential conversations that focus on the core aspects of strategy: (1) an improvement plan that frees up resources, (2) a growth plan that consumes resources, and (3) a risk management plan to govern the portfolio. This approach triggers a number of shifts.

The shift forces people to discuss growth plans without having to always discuss the "however." They can focus on where they can get to, and the resources required. So, you ask everyone for growth plans, possibly insisting on certain levels to make sure everyone is appropriately imaginative and aggressive. The same with an improvement plan. Only after you've had people put their best ideas on the table do you even begin to discuss risk.

The shift forces people to pay a lot of attention to the improvement plans, which often get swept aside by discussions on growth—and which, as we've seen, can produce big moves that lead to strategic success. By letting business leaders put risk explicitly on the table, you change their perception that their heads alone will be on the block if the strategic risk can't be mitigated. They will share what they know of their risks rather than hiding it in their plans—or not showing you an initiative at all because the personal risk is deemed to be too high.

Make risk versus growth trade-offs at a portfolio level. Most importantly, you can now aggregate all proposed initiatives regarding their growth contribution, improvement potential, and inherent risks. It is now possible for you to make decisions on how much risk you want the corporation to take on and to prioritize strategic moves according to a risk-return assessment on a portfolio level.

This is a big deal.

By separating the conversations, you force people to bring big moves on growth and improvements. You can now ask for audacious plans, say a plus-20 and a plus-40 plan. Then you have the explicit discussion about risk, you pool the risks for all plans, and you prioritize accordingly. You move from local optima with sandbags, to a corporate-wide optimum with well-understood risks.

You can then also have explicit discussions at the corporate level across all proposed initiatives about macroeconomic or geopolitical risk factors that rarely get explicitly recognized. You can ask, where relevant, for business leaders to submit a minus-20 or minus-40 plan. Then, they have no choice but to reflect risks that you might be concerned about.

Tailor approaches to different risk profiles. Too often we mix up apples and oranges when racking up projects. A "no-regret move" has known payoffs that work in all scenarios, for which standard NPV analysis does the trick perfectly. Often basic efficiency imperatives fit into this bucket. "Big bets" are high-commitment decisions that have a chance of being wrong. You must make them very carefully and apply a lot of scenario analysis and risk management. "Real options" have lower entry costs but longer-dated and more uncertain payoffs. Because they usually start out-of-the-money, a harsh, P&L-only view will kill them, so you will make too little investment in learning and optionality. Be disciplined and deliberate about discussing these different types of risk in different ways.

Adjust incentives to reflect risk. This shift, of course, has to translate into performance targets and incentive programs, as well. You will have to adjust the targets of leaders who do not get their initiatives approved, perhaps because they would have incurred risks that the company did not want to take. Having a very deliberate management of incentives clears the way for big moves.

7. From "you are your numbers" . . . to a holistic performance view

As hard as all the change will be, there is another complication: Whatever you do, you will not be able to do it alone. You will need to bring your team along.

You would not believe how often we see managers being pushed to accept "stretch targets," perhaps at best a P50 plan—only 50 percent chance of being achieved—and how absolutely forgotten these probabilities are when it comes to the performance review at year-end. People know that they "are their numbers," and they react accordingly to attempts to set targets. How can they not?

"WE WERE GOING FOR A HOCKEY STICK BUT WE GOT THE PUCK."

Of course, "inviting Mr. Bayes into the strategy room," i.e., bringing probabilities to the fore, can help change the dialogue. Discussing the 1-in-10 and the probabilities of success will change the frame and the perspective of your team. However, you will not get very far beyond a novelty effect if you do not go all the way to aligning incentives and to achieving a real shift in mindset with your team. Unless there is a sense of shared ownership for the fortunes of the company, you will have a hard time getting the full commitment of your team to the big moves required to mobilize your business.

A HOLISTIC PERFORMANCE VIEW

- Encourage noble failures, and focus on quality of effort
- Reflect higher or lower probabilities of success in your incentive structures
- Use team incentives over longer time-horizons in riskier contexts

Encourage noble failures. Clearly, understanding the probabilities of success is foundational. You need to have a sense of whether you are accepting a P30, a P50, or a P95 plan. This understanding forms the basis for a reasonable conversation at the end of the year of whether you are looking at a noble failure or a performance failure.

Naturally, developing this understanding requires you to dig down on what drove the outcomes—and, importantly, not do that just for failures. It's equally important to understand the causes of successes. You don't want to punish noble failures, but you also don't want to reward dumb luck. You want to motivate true quality of effort.

At Gore-Tex, for instance, teams get data on performance, and a vote is done on whether the team and its leader "did the right thing." This vote is often closer to the truth of what happened than the data themselves.

However you improve your understanding of probabilities and use them in incentives, it is crucial for people to understand that they won't be punished simply because a high-risk plan didn't pan out. To beat the odds, you have to overcome the approach that negotiates targets and then ruthlessly applies consequences based on outcomes. If you manage to instill a sense of shared ownership in your team, you will be off to a head start.

Reflect probabilities in incentive plans. We aren't suggesting you go to a "balanced score card," which just opens the field for new social games. Balanced scorecards inevitably create enough opportunities for emphasis that, as a team, you never know what somebody is most focused on delivering.

Instead, we propose an "unbalanced score card." This has two distinct halves: On the left is a common set of rolling financials with a focus on two or three, such as growth and ROI, that connect up to the economic profit goals of the division and enterprise. On the right are a set of strategically relevant initiatives and actions that underpin the plan. Here is how the incentive works: Your economic profit determines a 0–100 percent range for incentives. Then, each of the strategic changes can be a "knock-out" at the discretion of the "evaluator." In other words, the way you got the results matters as much as the results. And a knock-out is a knockout. Each factor can knock your bonus out, but there is human judgment, too: P50 moves will be treated more softly on failure than P90 moves. Could that change the game? It would certainly force a new conversation!

Play as a team. Some tasks have short time-horizons, have a very obvious link between activity and outcome, are easily monitored, and allow only a small role for luck. In these cases, detailed KPIs with heavy individual incentives probably make sense. But for many other tasks, there can be real problems because of time lags, cooperative effort, and "noisy" outcomes. That's why foreign exchange traders have very strong individual incentives but school teachers don't.

In particular, if you want good results from a portfolio of moves, you need to encourage enough risk-taking at the individual level so the total risk profile of the portfolio is optimized. As we know, in too many cases, individual risk aversion often prevails and the riskier moves get whittled out, even if they would make the average team performance much better. That's why, as risk goes up, you want individuals to be rewarded based on team performance. Of course there is a balance, because you don't want free riders. You need assurance that the right work is getting done, but in general, if you want more risk to get taken, then put a bigger shared component into individual incentives.

8. From long-range planning . . . to forcing the first step

We see it all the time: Even founders, chairmen, big CEOs, and some of the most impressive business leaders get stuck. They get plans that think big and excite them. They have grand visions of outcomes and performance levels. Industry leadership is presumed. But many of them run into a problem: There is no link between that grand vision and those bold aspirations to a real strategy, no link to the actual big moves that it will take to achieve the vision, and, in particular, no link to the first step it takes to get under way in the right direction. It is great to send someone out to achieve a vision, but how do you know what they will do next?

Most managers will listen to the visions, develop incremental plans that they deem doable, and execute as well as they can. Often, those plans get the company onto a path—but not one that reaches to the vision, nor to the full potential of their business.

To get to the end of a strategy execution, there has to be a beginning—a first step. That means that, after identifying your big moves, you must break them down into proximate goals, missions that are realistically achievable within a meaningful timeframe, say, 6–12 months. Asking the team to wind back goals into smaller, doable steps will not only force the team to get very practical about what to do next but also give you a road map to check whether they are on track to success.

FORCING THE FIRST STEP

- Put disproportionate focus on the first step when discussing long-term plans
- Roll back the future into 6-month increments and set proximate goals around clear operational metrics
- At first, focus more on actions than results
- Match and mobilize the required resources immediately

Focus on the first step. It's easy to confuse long-range planning with long-range actions. We leave the room with a warm glow about all the things we are going to do—one day. But we know the only thing we can really control is what is done now, and this is the sharp point of strategy.

Roll back the future. Rather than getting stuck imagining the destination, work back from there and set the milestone markers. Break the journey down into 6-month increments. Then test: Is what I need to do in the *first* 6 months actually possible? If the first step isn't doable, the rest of the plan is bunk. In the language of strategy professor Richard Rumelt, one of the true arts of strategy is determining the "proximate goal"—the best thing I can do now with my available capabilities and constraints to advance my strategy.[6]

At first, focus more on actions than results. The initial check-in on the plan should be more about whether the first steps have been taken rather than "show me the money." Performance conversations focused excessively on financial results put too much emphasis on lagging indicators: a look in the rearview mirror. On the other hand, McKinsey's specialist turnaround and restructuring experts spend a lot more time checking to make sure that actions are taken and milestones reached—and, you guessed it, the results follow.

Mobilize early resources. You can cascade long-term goals into clear, operational metrics and check back on whether initiatives have been given appropriate resources. We cannot tell you how many times we discuss strategic initiatives with clients, such as new growth businesses, but when we ask them about staffing they say they don't have anybody. You might want to think about organizing a series of "agile sprints" to get initiatives moving, investing a lot of energy to get things out of the starting blocks.

We have shown that big moves are meaningful only if pursued consistently over an extended period. The reason for this eighth and final shift is that every big move starts with a first step. Making sure that resources and people are lined up against the key initiatives is maybe the most important step of all in getting your strategy to beat the odds.

An insurance CEO, for instance, worked on a vision with his team, which concluded there would be no paper in the insurance business in 10 years. Plausible, isn't it? When he asked for the annual plan, paper consumption in the next year was set to increase. He then mused to his team: To connect to our vision, would it be viable to be flat in paper next year and go down the next? Of course, the team could not say no, and by framing a first-step question the CEO forced the strategy!

The package deal

Now, that was a lot of practical advice. Too much? Well, maybe, but we assure you that we have seen it all in motion—and it works.

The thing is, these eight shifts are a package deal. You cannot do some of them and not do others. There is a certain logic to them. Besides, the social side is a beast. You have to go all-in and do all of them together or you open the playing field for new social games. It takes a real intervention to jolt your team into this new frame.

How to do it? You will most likely find your very own way of doing it that suits your style, position, team, and business context. But let us illustrate in a simplified example how you might want to think about it: What if you adopted a new strategy process, reserving 10 days a year for conversations and introducing the shifts one meeting at a time? Could that work?

If things went wrong, you would go wrong only in one place and could then course-correct for the next conversation. Let's presume, for instance, that at the end of the 10 days you have not been able to free up all the resources you feel are needed. Fine, you take this as a starting point. You take the resources you were able to free up by the end of this first planning cycle and allocate them to the highest-priority businesses.

That's a start, and, more importantly, your team now understands what this new process is all about. That allows you to then increase the level of resources you demand over time.

Here is the outline of a 10-day schedule, spread over whatever period of time you think would be right:

- **Days 1 and 2:** Kickoff meeting to start the journey; discuss the list of strategic topics you need to address; discuss the momentum case; sequence the topics across the other 8 days; announce the free resources needed for the cycle.
- **Day 3:** Describe real alternatives for each strategic topic; start the debate on direction; identify the major choices to make; update the list of strategic topics and discussion sequence.
- **Day 4:** Describe alternatives for big moves in each business, again; update the list of strategic topics and discussion sequence.
- **Day 5:** Deepen the discussion on priority topics (follow sequence); start picking the 1-in-10s; sort plans into the P50s and the P90s; take your first votes; update the list of strategic topics and discussion sequence.
- **Day 6:** Deepen the discussion on priority topics (follow sequence); describe the big moves for each business; make the 1-in-10 picks; update the list of strategic topics and discussion sequence.
- **Day 7:** Deepen the discussion on priority topics (follow sequence); discuss the big moves as a portfolio of growth initiatives, improvement initiatives, and risks involved; choose the moves to be pursued with a portfolio view; update the list of strategic topics and discussion sequence.
- **Days 8 and 9:** Deepen the discussion on priority topics (follow sequence); translate the plan into unbalanced score cards; workshop the key success factors and failure modes and develop mitigation plans; commit the team; update the list of strategic topics and discussion sequence.
- **Day 10:** Finalize the first steps; zoom in on details for the first 6 months; take stock and update the ongoing list of strategic topics and discussion sequence; celebrate!

What do you think? Wouldn't this process be much more real—and a lot more fun—than the usual hockey sticks and peanut butter business?

Epilogue

New life in the strategy room

Are you ready to give big moves a chance?

O r does that all sound just a bit too easy?
    Well, maybe. Strategy remains hard work, and good strategy takes a lot of creativity. Executing strategies requires determined and resilient leadership. Only then do companies have a chance of moving up the Power Curve.

However, in all that we have seen in strategy rooms and boardrooms around the world over our decades of spending time with CEOs, even if you show those three crucial attributes—hard work, new ideas, and resilience—that's not enough. The social side of strategy will likely get in the way. It pulls down good ideas. It produces under-resourced hockey sticks, spreads peanut butter, and leads to disappointing outcomes—for everybody involved.

You have to turn to the empirics of strategy and have a realistic outside view. Only then can you change the context and have more honest discussions in the strategy room.

You can then have the chance to create consensus about strategic decisions that commit to big moves. You are more likely to be fair in terms of the incentives you create for your teams and to differentiate correctly between how much of performance depends on what's happening in the industry and how much credit or blame should go to an individual. You have a chance to create incentives that get everyone to act in the best interests of the corporation and its stakeholders—rather than ultimately just in their own interests. In short, you have a shot at creating a better life and better outcomes for everybody involved.

With this book, we hope to have shed some light for you on the fabric of good business strategy, on what truly works and what doesn't. We hope we've made a tangible contribution to how you think about strategy by identifying the levers that contribute most to successes and failures. You can now combine these into calibrating your own strategy against a vast set of companies and their actual journeys. Most important, we hope that reading this book has given you a lot of practical inspiration on how to change the way you use facts in your strategy room (and boardroom) to beat the social side of strategy.

"WE DID AWAY WITH THE SOCIAL SIDE OF STRATEGY."

Strategy remains part science, part art—but with the underlying research of this book, we now have the understanding and the tools to effectively address some of the perennial conundrums around mobilizing management teams and companies. If you embrace the idea of probability, and internalize the ideas of this book about strategy to beat the odds, you might find your own way of overcoming human biases and addressing the social side of strategy. We are confident that, if you do, you will have a better shot at beating the market and creating value for your stakeholders.

Hey, why not? Let's make it happen!

Acknowledgments

Our Clients—for whom we have the utmost respect for trying and testing over the years so many of the insights summarized in this book—and who generously shared their wisdom with us.

Our Partners at McKinsey—for placing their confidence in us and investing over the years to help create a unique set of insights that reframe strategy—to go "where nobody has gone before."

Nicholas Northcote—for four years of leadership in the analytical work and countless hours in the strategy room with us, battling out the insights and the story of the book . . . and managing to not get knocked out, as with his real-world boxing experience.

Paul Carroll—the only one who actually knew how to write a book.

Patrick Viguerie—for having been part of the team for a long time and providing early inspiration.

Angus Dawson—who was on the journey going right back to *Granularity of Growth.*

Bibi Smit, Sabine Hirt, and Mel Bradley—for their wisdom and patience—but even more so for their and our families' unwavering support in situations when the effort appeared to become unending. Special thanks also to Sabine for all the hands-on feedback about the manuscript.

Our McKinsey support teams over the last 3 years: Andre Fromyhr, Eleanor Bensley, and Lucy Wark during the book-creation phase; and Bhawna Gupta, Roerich Bansal, Vikram Khanna, Zack Taylor, Patryk Strojny, Sven Kämmerer, Enrique Gomez Serrano, and Wladimir Nikoluk while we were developing the analytical concepts and fact base.

Bhawna Gupta and her team—for building the models and spending countless hours cleaning the numbers and supporting hundreds of CEO conversations over the years.

Tim Koller, Werner Rehm, Bin Jiang, Marc de Jong, and their teams at McKinsey's Strategy Analytics Centre—for many inspiring conversations over the years and for having built a unique set of corporate performance analytics assets.

Victoria Newman, Blair Warner, Tammy Anson-Smith, Nicole Sallmann, Philippa Hazlitt, and Jennifer Chiang—for their feedback and for their support of our service lines and reach and relevance efforts.

Jeremy Banks and Mike Shapiro—for bringing our script to life with their cartoons.

The thought leaders behind a number of the crucial strategic insights, especially Michael Birshan, Dan Lovallo, and Stephen Hall (resource re-allocation); Bill Huyett, Andy West, and Robert Uhlaner (value creation in M&A); Erik Roth, Marc de Jong, and Gordon Orr (innovation); and Ezra Greenberg and our colleagues from the McKinsey Global Institute (trends). And, outside the firm, we were inspired by the work of Dan Ariely, Daniel Kahneman, John Roberts, Phil Rosenzweig, Richard Rumelt, Nassim Nicholas Taleb, Philip Tetlock, Richard Thaler, and others

Allen Webb, Rik Kirkland, Joanna Pachner, and Joshua Dowse—for their guidance and editorial contributions. And to James Newman and Nicole White from McKinsey Sydney Design Studio, who made our graphics.

The hundreds of our Partner colleagues around the world who have trusted us with their client Chairmen and CEOs in countless inspiring meetings.

Appendix

This appendix covers: (1) our sample and method; (2) a note on economic profit and total returns to shareholders; and (3) what is different if a firm starts at the top or the bottom, versus the focus in the body of the book on mobility from the middle.

1. About our sample and method

The results in this paper come from a multi-year McKinsey & Company research effort to quantitatively and objectively assess the likelihood that a strategy would deliver on its promise to beat the market. We didn't want to produce another framework; we wanted to find out how to beat the odds.

Our data source. This outside view is based on a rigorous statistical analysis of the biggest reliable data set we could muster: the 3,925 largest-revenue, non-financial companies in our proprietary McKinsey Corporate Performance Analytics company database, spanning 15 years, 59 industries, and 73 countries.

Time periods. Our sample was divided into three 5-year time periods: 2000–4, 2005–9, and 2010–14. To get rid of noise, we averaged economic profits within those periods, counting in the sample if there were enough data for at least 3 of those 5 years. We have recalculated the model several times across different starting points (one of the luxuries of this book taking so long to build), and the results have been extremely robust to these time shifts.

The sample. For our time periods, 2,393 companies had sufficient data to track their movement on the Power Curve over time; meaning, economic profit was calculable for 3 out of 5 years in both 2000–4 and 2010–14. This resulted in a sample that spanned three 5-year periods, 59 industries, and 62 countries—and is used as the consistent reference point across the book. The final sample of 2,393 companies had median revenues of $5.2 billion in 2010–14, with an average of $12.4 billion and a range of $0.7 billion to $458.0 billion. Of the final sample, only 101 are above $50 billion and only 31 companies fell above

$100 billion. The sample is also very global. Asia leads the list with 945 firms, followed by North America (744), Europe (552), South America (72), and the rest of the world (80).

Calculating economic profit. Economic profit was calculated based on McKinsey's proprietary Corporate Performance Analytics data, which ensures a clean and "apples to apples" data set across companies, jurisdictions, and time. The method is consistent with our widely read text *Valuation*: subtracting the capital charge (invested capital multiplied by the weighted average cost of capital, or WACC) from net operating profit less adjusted taxes (NOPLAT). Our calculation for WACC was based on global industry betas. However, given that (most) companies earn profit in local currency, an artificial weakening or strengthening of the exchange rate to USD will make changes in economic profit look too big or too small. Therefore, a conversion factor based on the average inflation differential between currencies over the period has been applied to convert economic profits into USD.

Industry classifications. We used the accepted standard for industry classification, the Global Industry Classification Standard, which was developed by S&P Dow Jones Indices. The four-tiered GICS structure consists of 11 sectors, 24 industry groups, 68 industries, and 157 sub-industries. Taking the middle two levels as the most meaningful for descriptive purposes, both the original database of 3,925 companies and the final set of 2,393 data-sufficient companies spanned 20 industry groups and 59 industries.

The odds model. For each of these 2,393 companies, we gathered publicly available data on their actions (for example, from Deal Logic), summarized into 40 scoring variables. We then employed a multinomial logistical regression model to estimate the contribution of these 40 possible scoring variables to the probability of moving up and down the Power Curve. Our algorithms sorted these into 10 variables that, together, produced the most statistically significant and efficient regression model.

Predictive power. To test the accuracy of our model, we used a "receiver operating characteristic" or ROC curve, for which scores of over 80 percent are considered to be a strong predictive result. Our analysis tracks moves between 2004 and 2014, for which the ROC score is 82.8. This means that for any pair of an upwardly mobile firm and a non-upwardly mobile firm, our model gave higher odds to the upwardly mobile firm 82.8 percent of the time. Despite this high score, predictive models based on historical data can reflect noise in the historical data as much as the tested variables and are prone to overfitting. We therefore ran our model across different time periods and still yielded a ROC score of at least 78 percent. So, while our results are derived from backward-looking data, we are confident that they are meaningful for forward-looking forecasts.

2. A note on economic profit and total returns to shareholders

Total return to shareholders will only differ from the risk-adjusted cost of equity when there is a surprise factor. Therefore, to understand the impact of performance on share price, one must account for what was expected to begin with.

To do so, we collected our sample into a 5 × 5 matrix: one axis cutting into quintiles for the average enterprise value/NOPLAT multiple in the starting multiple, the other for the subsequent evolution of economic profit (scaled relative to starting size). See Exhibit A1.

When we do this, we see very clearly that the best place to be is to have low expectations and deliver high performance—and the worst is to do just the opposite. However, the matrix also shows that for an executive, starting with low expectations matters just as much as delivering breakthrough performance.

The other clear takeaway is that growth in economic profit, no matter the starting multiple, generates higher returns for shareholders. The highest performers delivered 17 percent total returns over the period, while those in the bottom 60 percent of improvers delivered just 7 percent.

3. How the odds look different from the top or bottom

We've made general observations about endowment, trends, and moves based on the experience of companies in the middle quintiles,

Exhibit A1

Total returns to shareholders
TRS depends both on what you delivered and what was first expected

---

		Starting multiple quintile[2] At 2000-04						
		Lowest	II	III	IV	Highest	All	
EP growth[1] quintile Over decade to 2010-2014	Highest	25	21	18	13	9	17	
	IV	19	14	13	8	8	12	
	III	15	9	5	5	4	7	
	II	11	8	6	4	5	7	
	Lowest	11	7	6	2	1	7	
	All	16	11	9	7	6	10	Full sample average

---

1 Calculated as change in EP, scaled by starting IC

2 Calculated as NEV/NOPLAT

Source: McKinsey Corporate Performance Analytics™

but, of course, that's not where everyone lives. In fact, by definition, 40 percent of companies don't, with half of those in the doldrums and half of them where we all want to be, in that top quintile. And, yes, there are important differences if you aren't starting in the middle.

If you start in the middle you have just an 8 percent chance of ending in the top quintile, while starting in the top quintile gives you a 59 percent chance of staying there.

Perhaps more useful is knowing that the thresholds and impacts of the 10 mobility attributes vary depending on your starting position. Looking at size, for example, the definition of what "large" is changes slightly, and being large has a different impact on your odds profile depending on your starting point. As a middle company, you're large if your revenue is in the top 20 percent of companies. At the top, you need to be in the top 10 percent, and at the bottom you only need to be in the top 30 percent. When you start in the middle, being a large company improves your odds of moving to the top quintile from 8 percent to 23 percent. When you're at the top, being large improves your odds of staying there from 59 percent to 74 percent. When you're at the bottom, being large only improves your odds of moving up the curve (to the middle or top) from 57 percent to 61 percent.

Life at the top

For companies starting in the top quintile (Exhibit A2), making a big move by increasing capex doesn't have a statistically significant impact on the odds of mobility. That's not to say that, once you're at the top, you can cease capital expenditures; it's just that being so far ahead of your industry on capex won't necessarily improve your odds of staying in the top group. The group of star companies already in the top quintile may have already demonstrated sufficient investment opportunities to grow economic profit, so growing the capital base further doesn't move the needle. Or, the well of investment opportunities whose returns will be better than cost of capital has started to dry up in the industries where the star companies operate.

Instead of moving big on capex, companies in the top quintile are better served by the other big moves to defend their lofty status on the Power Curve (scouting for acquisitions, re-allocating their resources to the optimal uses, innovating their business model, and especially improving productivity). Productivity is the most important big move when starting at the top because the scale of invested capital and high ROIC have already got you there, and it's much more difficult to find accretive investments (acquisitions, capex re-allocation, or growth projects) that really move the needle.

Life at the bottom

For companies starting in the bottom quintile (Exhibit A3), past R&D expenditure doesn't appear to change the odds of moving up the curve. For bottom companies, the strongest swing factors are the industry trend and capital expenditure, and you want to avoid being in the bottom decile of differentiation improvement.

Exhibit A2

The odds from the top

Top-quintile firms have a 59% chance of staying at the top

Percent chance of remaining in top
N = 479 firms in the top quintile, rank-ordered

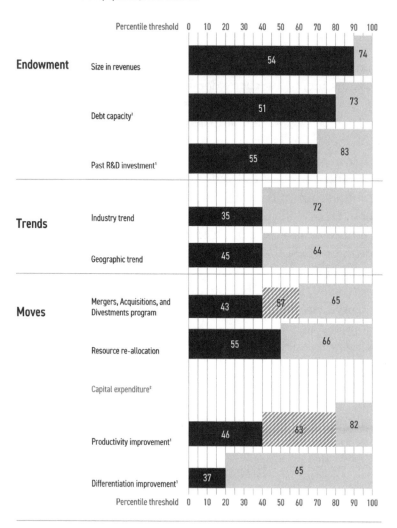

1 Normalized by industry median

2 Level of capital expenditure does not have a statistically significant effect on mobility for firms starting in the top quintile

Source: McKinsey Corporate Performance Analytics™

Exhibit A3

The odds from the bottom

Bottom-quintile firms have a 57% chance of moving out of the bottom

---

Percent chance of moving out of the bottom
N = 479 firms in the bottom quintile, rank-ordered

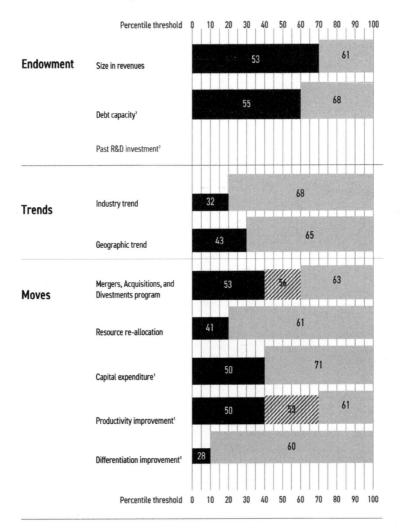

1 Normalized by industry median

2 Past R&D investment does not have a statistically significant effect on upwards mobility for firms starting in the bottom quintile

Source: McKinsey Corporate Performance Analytics™

But overall, as much as there are differences around the edges depending on where you start on the Power Curve—and they are big—the overwhelmingly consistent theme is that there are ten attributes that matter in determining your odds of moving up the curve. Regardless of your starting position, you have an advantage with better endowment; the trends will push and pull you over time, and you should adapt to them the best you can; and you should make as many big moves as you can relative to competition. The fact that life is different at the top, in the middle, or at the bottom was not in the strategy room. Now it can be.

Notes

Introduction. Welcome to the strategy room

1. A list of the favorite strategy books among leaders of our firm's strategy practice, according to a recent email trail where one of our new offices wanted advice on what should get space on their bookshelves, includes: *Strategy: A History* (Lawrence Freedman, 2013), *The Innovator's Dilemma: When New Technologies Cause Great Firms to Fail* (Clayton Christensen, 1997), *Good Strategy/Bad Strategy: The Difference and Why It Matters* (Richard Rumelt, 2011), *The Art of War* (Sun Tzu, 5th Century BC), *Co-opetition: A Revolutionary Mindset That Combines Competition and Cooperation* (Adam M. Brandenburger and Barry J. Nalebuff, 1996), and *The Lords of Strategy: The Secret Intellectual History of the New Corporate World* (Walter Kiechel III, 2010). Aside from these mainstream tomes, the list also included books only tangentially related to strategy such as *Antifragile: Things That Gain from Disorder* (Nassim Nicholas Taleb, 2012), *The Signal and the Noise: Why So Many Predictions Fail—but Some Don't* (Nate Silver, 2012), and *Thinking, Fast and Slow* (Daniel Kahneman, 2011). And the list goes right back to the historical military roots of strategy, from 1776 with *Decline and Fall of the Roman Empire* (Edward Gibbon, 1776), *On War* (Carl von Clausewitz, 1832), and *The Strategy of Conflict* (Thomas Shelling's classic from 1981).
2. Widely attributed to the management guru Peter Drucker.
3. For a summary of the inside view versus the outside view, see "Beware the inside view," *McKinsey Quarterly*, November 2011, on McKinsey.com, where Nobel Laureate Daniel Kahneman relates his story about where this idea first dawned on him. For a deeper treatment, where he surveys the broader field of behavioral economics in great style, see Daniel Kahneman, *Thinking, Fast and Slow*, New York: Farrar, Straus and Giroux, 2011.
4. See Phillip Tetlock, *Expert Political Judgment: How Good Is It? How Can We Know?*, Princeton, NJ: Princeton University Press, 2005. Tetlock's multi-year, longitudinal competition on expert predictions pitted political scientists and international relations scholars against each other in a quest for accuracy. The competition led him to conclude that the more famous an expert forecaster, the more overconfident they were. "Experts in demand," Tetlock says, "were more overconfident than their colleagues who eked out existences far from the limelight."
5. To learn more about our model, please see the Appendix.

Chapter 1. Games in the strategy room—and why people play them

1. These are archetypical business school case studies of the Innovator's Dilemma: players with a comfortable-to-dominant market share and market-leading technologies, who failed to recognize or react to the disruption of a new technology. For the original expression of this concept, see Clayton Christensen, *The Innovator's Dilemma: When New Technologies Cause Great Firms to Fail*, Boston: Harvard Business School Press, 1997.

2. SWOT is an acronym for Strengths, Weaknesses, Opportunities, and Threats—a common planning framework in use for the last few decades to assess the internal advantages and disadvantages as well as the positive and negative external forces.

3. See Chris Bradley, Angus Dawson, and Antoine Montard, "Mastering the building blocks of strategy," *McKinsey Quarterly*, October 2013. In this piece, we articulated four methods to get to great strategy: do justice to the building blocks, myth-bust your own story, let them grapple, and don't leave the strategy unfinished. The point on myth-busting was further built on in Bradley's subsequent blog: Chris Bradley, "Strategists as myth-busters: Why you shouldn't believe your own stories," LinkedIn, 2016.

4. See Jack Welch and John Byrne's *Jack: Straight from the Gut*, New York: Warner Books, 2003.

5. Also known as "Joy's Law," the statement is widely attributed to Sun Microsystems co-founder Bill Joy.

6. See Daniel Kahneman, *Thinking, Fast and Slow*, New York: Farrar, Straus and Giroux, 2011. For a neat summary of the particular story about the Israeli textbook project in this paragraph, refer to Daniel Kahneman's excerpt: "Beware the inside view," *McKinsey Quarterly*, November 2011.

7. See again Phillip Tetlock, *Expert Political Judgment: How Good Is It? How Can We Know?*, Princeton, NJ: Princeton University Press, 2005. Tetlock's multi-year, longitudinal competition on expert predictions, pitting political scientists and international relations scholars against each other in a quest for accuracy, led him to conclude that experts tend to use a double standard in assessing information: They were much tougher in assessing the validity of information that undercut their theory than they were concerning information that supported it. Also see Philip Tetlock and Dan Gardner, *Superforecasting: The Art and Science of Prediction*, New York: Broadway Books, 2015. The second book details findings from an expert prediction competition known as the Good Judgment Project, otherwise known as the IARPA (Intelligence Advanced Research Projects Agency) tournament, which ran from 2011 to 2015. In the book, Tetlock takes a more optimistic line on the possibility of accurate forecasting by identifying the characteristics of highly successful forecasters.

8. See Larry Swedroe, "Why you should ignore economic forecasts," *CBS Money Watch*, November 26, 2012.

9. This is true for only two of the three authors; one does not yet have much gray hair at all and still looks like a fresh grad.

10. These results are drawn from a survey of 159 Chief Strategy Officers on the strategy process that we ran in 2014 as part of the research for this book.

11. There are some great popular books published by the actual pioneers of this burgeoning field, allowing the everyday reader to get a first-hand account. The three first picks for us are: Daniel Kahneman, *Thinking, Fast and Slow*, New York: Farrar, Straus and Giroux, 2011; Dan Ariely, *Predictably Irrational: The Hidden Forces That Shape Our Decisions*, New York: Harper Perennial, 2010; and Richard Thaler, *Misbehaving: The Making of Behavioral Economics*, New York: Norton, 2015.

12. See Eric Johnson and Daniel Goldstein's original 2004 study, "Defaults and donation decisions," in *Transplantation*, 2004, Vol. 78, No. 12, 1713–1716. This, along with many other important contributions to behavioral economics, is featured in Dan Ariely's *Predictably Irrational: The Hidden Forces That Shape Our Decisions*, New York: HarperPerennial, 2010.

13. See Phil Rosenzweig, *The Halo Effect and the Eight Other Business Delusions That Deceive Managers*, New York: Free Press, 2007. In this important book, Rosenzweig makes the point that too often we rush to connect observed practices with results, leading to the dangerous conclusion that "if I do X, then I will also get that result, too." While we logically understand that cherry-picking examples, applying loose causation, and ignoring sampling and survivor bias is going to lead to poor decisions, it's interesting to see how prevalent these thought mistakes are not just in boardrooms but in management books and articles, too.

14. For more on champion bias, see Tim Koller, Dan Lovallo, and Zane Williams's article "A bias against investment?," *McKinsey Quarterly*, 2011.

15. See Dominic Dodd and Ken Favaro, *The Three Tensions: Winning the Struggle to Perform Without Compromise*, San Francisco: Jossey-Bass, 2007.

16. See, for example, Drew Westen's ground-breaking work on confirmation bias in political reasoning: Drew Westen, Pavel Blagov, Keith Harenski, Clint Kilts, and Stephan Hamann, "Neural bases of motivated reasoning: An fMRI study of emotional constraints on partisan political judgment in the 2004 US presidential election," *Journal of Cognitive Neuroscience*, 2006, Vol. 18, 1947–1958.

17. The concept of survivor bias owes much to the work of Abraham Wald and his Statistical Research Group division of the US Navy during World War II. Survivor bias consists of creating a data set to explain a phenomenon that includes only the visible remaining observations— "survivors"—rather than the full set of possible observations. While working

on the problem of how to minimize bomber losses to enemy fire, the SRG recognized that aircraft that had survived their missions had been hit in less critical spots, and recommended reinforcing the areas of the plane where they had not been hit. The Navy's inclination was to reinforce areas where the planes had been hit, but Wald and his team made an assumption of uniform damage, which led them to conclude that planes hit in other places were being lost at far higher rates than those that sustained damage but ultimately survived the enemy fire. In a sad irony, Wald and his wife eventually perished in a plane crash in the Nilgiri mountains during a lecture tour of India.

18. We take this colorful term from Nassim Taleb's *The Black Swan: The Impact of the Highly Improbable*, New York: Random House, 2007. Taleb writes: "More than two thousand years ago, the Roman orator, belletrist, thinker, Stoic, manipulator-politician, and (usually) virtuous gentleman, Marcus Tullius Cicero, presented the following story. One Diagoras, a nonbeliever in the gods, was shown painted tablets bearing the portraits of some wor-shippers who prayed, then survived a subsequent shipwreck. The implication was that praying protects you from drowning. Diagoras asked, 'Where were the pictures of those who prayed, then drowned?'"

19. The principal-agent problem as currently understood in a business context grew out of the combination of economics and institutional theory by certain academics, such as Stephen Ross, Michael Jensen, William Meckling, John Roberts, and others in the 1970s and 1980s. Their work built on earlier studies in game theory on incentive compatibility problems under asymmetric infor-mation. The problem emerges when an agent is required to make decisions for another person or group, whose information, preferences, and interests may not be aligned with the agent's. Situations where their interests diverge are often described as involving "moral hazard."

    A seminal academic contribution was Michael Jensen's and William Meckling's work elaborating how agency costs are generated by the exis-tence of outside debt and equity that are not linked as directly to managers' interests as to owners' interests. See "Theory of the firm: Managerial behavior, agency costs and ownership structure," *Journal of Financial Economics*, October 1976, Vol. 3, No. 4, 305–360.

    John Roberts elegantly summarized and applied many of these ideas for business organizations in the influential book *The Modern Firm* (New York: Oxford University Press, 2004), which *The Economist* cited as the best business book of that year.

20. This quote is attributed widely to the famous pair of collaborators and investors. Another version of this quote we found: "The finance industry is 5 percent rational people and 95 percent shamans and faith healers."

21. See Stephen Hall, Dan Lovallo, and Reinier Musters, "How to put your money where your strategy is," *McKinsey Quarterly*, March 2012. This has

been a theme in the McKinsey strategy practice. See, for example, these follow-up articles: Yuval Atsmon, "How nimble resource allocation can double your company's value," August 2016; Stephen Hall and Conor Kehoe, "Breaking down the barriers to corporate resource allocation," October 2013; Michael Birshan, Marja Engel, and Oliver Sibony, "Avoiding the quicksand: Ten techniques for more agile corporate resource allocation," October 2013.

22. On the complicated reasons for Kodak's failure to change in the face of technological revolution, see this excellent piece revisiting a well-trodden area of business lore: Willy Shih, "The real lessons from Kodak's decline," MIT *Sloan Management Review*, Summer 2016.

Chapter 2. Opening the windows of your strategy room

1. The Fra Mauro map, considered one of the greatest and most detailed examples of medieval cartography, was created in the mid-fifteenth century over the course of several years by a Venetian monk. It measures about two by two meters, and is oriented south-end-up. The map is usually displayed at Museo Correr in Venice.

2. The sixteenth-century mapmaker Diogo Ribeiro's most important work is considered to be the 1529 Padrón Real. There are six copies attributed to Ribeiro, including the Weimar version pictured in this text, hosted at (what was originally known as) the Weimar Grand Ducal Library. The Spanish-Portuguese rivalry for control of the spice trade and Magellan's first global circumnavigation in 1522 shaped the map; control of the valuable Moluccas Islands would be determined by the map's "objective" depiction of the globe, but the Portuguese Ribeiro switched sides and was paid by the Spanish to show the islands just within the Spanish half.

3. See Yuval Noah Harari, *Sapiens: A Brief History of Humankind*, New York: HarperCollins, 2015.

4. The power curve analysis was first featured in Chris Bradley, Angus Dawson, and Sven Smit, "The strategic yardstick you can't afford to ignore," *McKinsey Quarterly*, October 2013.

5. See Chris Bradley, Martin Hirt, and Sven Smit, "Have you tested your strategy lately?," *McKinsey Quarterly*, January 2011.

6. Economic value added (EVA) is also known as economic profit. It's a measure of financial performance calculated by deducting a company's cost of capital from its operating profit adjusted for taxes. For more, see Tim Koller, Marc Goedhart, David Wessels, and Thomas Copeland, *Valuation: Measuring and Managing the Value of Companies*, Hoboken, NJ: John Wiley & Sons, 2005.

7. See the Appendix for a more detailed chart on the relationship between economic profit and total shareholder return. On the subject of valuation in corporate finance, see Tim Koller, Marc Goedhart, David Wessels, and Thomas Copeland, *Valuation: Measuring and Managing the Value of Companies*, Hoboken, NJ: John Wiley & Sons, 2005; and Tim Koller, Richard Dobbs, and Bill Huyett, *Value: The Four Cornerstones of Corporate Finance*, Hoboken, NJ: John Wiley & Sons, 2011. To understand how our Firm looks at total returns to shareholders, refer to Bas Deelder, Marc H. Goedhart, and Ankur Agrawal, "A better way to understand TRS," *McKinsey Quarterly*, July 2008.

8. We measure profit as NOPLAT—Net Operating Profit Less Adjusted Taxes. Invested capital comprises operating invested capital of $6.6 billion and goodwill and intangibles of $2.6 billion. In other words, 28 percent of the capital of a typical company represents additional value over book value paid in acquisitions. Executives often prefer measures excluding goodwill, arguing this is a truer representation of operational performance and incremental returns. We are biased to including goodwill. First, the empirical reality is that a good share of corporate growth has come, and will come, from acquisitions and therefore the post-goodwill returns are a better measure of the true situation. Second, that goodwill was real cash spent by a real investor and still needs a return.

9. "Power law" refers to a functional relationship between two quantities, where a relative change in one quantity results in a proportional relative change in the other quantity, independent of the initial size of those quantities: One quantity varies as a power of another. Power laws are found commonly throughout the natural and social sciences, as well as in various fields of industry. For example, phenomena described with power laws include fractals, the initial mass of stars, the growth of city populations, and even returns to venture capital investment.

10. The 2,393 companies are the ones also with sufficient contiguous data to complete our study. See the Appendix for further details on sample composition.

11. In general, Zipf's Law describes a pattern where the frequency of an item or event is inversely proportional to its frequency rank. The use of words in the English language is one such example.

12. Here are the top 40 for 2010–14 in order: Apple, Microsoft, China Mobile, Samsung Electronics, Exxon, Johnson & Johnson, Oracle, Roche, BHP, Vodafone, Intel, Cisco, Pfizer, GlaxoSmithKline, Novartis, AstraZeneca, Nestlé, Chevron, Merck, Walmart, Coca-Cola, Qualcomm, CNOOC, BAT, Telefonica, UnitedHealth, Gilead, Sanofi, America Movil, TSMC, PetroChina, Anheuser-Busch, Audi, PepsiCo, Abbott, Unilever, Verizon, Altria, Amgen, Siemens. The list comprises 11 pharma/biotech firms, 8 consumer companies, 8 tech firms, 5 global resource players (who have

slid down the list since 2014 given the cyclical nature of commodity prices), 5 telecommunications carriers, a healthcare provider, a car maker, and an industrial manufacturer.

13. We are sometimes questioned about using total economic profit because some feel the measure skews the results too much to large companies, at the expense of smaller companies with high margins. But who is more valuable: a Major League Baseball player who bats .300 in 100 at-bats against right-handed pitchers or an everyday player who bats .285 in 550 at-bats? We know who we'd take.

Chapter 3. Hockey stick dreams, hairy back realities

1. See Dan Lovallo and Olivier Sibony, "The case for behavioral strategy," *McKinsey Quarterly*, March 2010.
2. For more information, see Chris Bradley's post "Hockey stick dreams, hairy back reality," *McKinsey Strategy and Corporate Finance Blog*, 2017.
3. See Ola Svenson's 1981 paper "Are we all less risky and more skillful than our fellow drivers?," *Acta Psychologica*, 1981, Vol. 47, No. 2, 143–148.
4. See Daniel Kahneman and Dan Lovallo, "Timid choices and bold forecasts: A cognitive perspective on risk taking," *Management Science*, January 1993, Vol. 39, No. 1, 17–31.
5. See our writing collaborator's book: Paul Carroll, *Big Blues: The Unmaking of IBM*, New York: Crown, 1993. Paul was a Wall Street journalist who had been covering IBM for years. The year this book was published, Lou Gerstner took over as CEO and began his now-famous turnaround of the company.
6. See Joshua Fenton, Anthony Jerant, Klea Bertakis, and Peter Franks, "The cost of satisfaction," *Archives of Internal Medicine*, 2012, Vol. 172, No. 5, 405–11.
7. Variations of the quote "prediction is difficult, especially about the future" are attributed to Danish Nobel Prize–winning physicist Niels Bohr and later to famous New York Yankees player and coach Yogi Berra.
8. See Nassim Taleb's *Fooled by Randomness: The Hidden Role of Chance in Life and in the Markets*, New York: Random House, 2005. Taleb coined the term "narrative fallacy" to describe the human tendency to understand complex sets of facts by transforming them into oversimplified narratives. It is important to note that this effect can undermine our judgment in two directions, worsening our ability to gauge future possibilities and past causation. In other words, we are afflicted by uncertainty both about what has happened and about what will happen next.
9. See Stephen Hall, Dan Lovallo, and Reinier Musters, "How to put your money where your strategy is," *McKinsey Quarterly*, March 2012.

Chapter 4. What are the odds?

1. For a good discussion of this, see our ex-colleague Yuval Atsmon's "How tales of triumphant underdogs lead strategists astray," *LinkedIn Blog*, May 2016.
2. One thing that you might have been wondering when studying the matrix is why it is more likely to move from the bottom to the top (17 percent chance), than to move from the middle to the top (8 percent chance). The explanation is that larger companies are slightly over-represented in the top and bottom quintiles. Given their scale, if they make a move in ROIC, it is more likely to catapult them all the way from the bottom to the top, rather than settling in the middle.
3. See, for example, *The Base Rate Book* by Michael Mauboussin, Dan Callahan, and Darius Majd of Credit Suisse, 2016. This resource—freely available online at the time of publication—racks up tables of probability distributions for growth and performance contingent on various population characteristics like size. It's a good example of bringing the "outside view" into strategy and investing.
4. Widely attributed to the 19-season National Football League (NFL) head coach. Bill Parcells coached the New York Giants to two Super Bowl titles and later served as the head coach of the New England Patriots, New York Jets, and Dallas Cowboys.
5. See "Staying one step ahead at Pixar: An interview with Ed Catmull," *McKinsey Quarterly*, March 2016.

Chapter 5. How to find the real hockey stick

1. See the classic piece by Louis V. Gerstner Jr., former CEO of IBM and McKinsey New York alumnus, "Can strategic planning pay off?," *McKinsey Quarterly*, December 1973. We reprinted this article in 2013 as part of a retrospective to celebrate the fiftieth anniversary of the *McKinsey Quarterly*. Even in 1973, he was comparing the revolutionary promise of strategic planning (the hot new management tool) with actual progress inside of companies. In a way that resonates with us 45 years later, he points out that the fundamental flaw is "the failure to bring strategic planning down to current decisions." He advises readers to "make decisions not plans," incorporate flexibility and uncertainty, ensure "top down leadership" not just a roll-up of bottom-up imperatives without considering linkages and trade-offs, and focus on "resource allocation decisions." We read this when our *McKinsey Quarterly* head Allen Webb found it from the archives, and were humbled that there is nothing new under the sun.
2. See Jennifer Rheingold and Ryan Underwood, "Was 'built to last' built to last?," *Fast Company*, 2014. Also see a recent analysis by one of the authors,

Chris Bradley, "What happened to the world's 'greatest' companies?," *McKinsey Strategy and Corporate Finance Blog*, September 2017.

3. See again Phil Rosenzweig's *The Halo Effect and the Eight Other Business Delusions That Deceive Managers*, New York: Free Press, 2007.

4. The reference is to Reverend Thomas Bayes, a statistician, philosopher, and Presbyterian minister who lived in the early to mid-1700s and developed an important statistical technique that allows estimates to become more precise as new information is incorporated.

5. See "Fading stars," *Economist*, February 27, 2016.

Chapter 6. The writing is on the wall

1. The ideas in this chapter draw on Chris Bradley and Clayton O'Toole, "An incumbent's guide to digital disruption," *McKinsey Quarterly*, May 2016. We're grateful to Clayton O'Toole, the co-author of that piece, for his assistance with the ideas in this chapter.

2. See Chris Bradley, Martin Hirt, and Sven Smit, "Have you tested your strategy lately?," *McKinsey Quarterly*, January 2011.

3. See Stephen Hall, Dan Lovallo, and Reinier Musters, "How to put your money where your strategy is," *McKinsey Quarterly*, March 2012.

4. See Patrick Viguerie, Sven Smit, and Mehrdad Baghai, *The Granularity of Growth: How to Identify the Sources of Growth and Drive Enduring Company Performance*, Hoboken, NJ: John Wiley & Sons, 2007.

5. World Economic Forum, Global entrepreneurship and successful growth strategies of early-stage companies report, April 2011.

6. See Reed Hastings, "An explanation and some reflections," *Netflix blog*, September 18, 2011. The interesting thing about this blog is that it was written as events were unfolding, so it is immune from the "selective memory" of history.

7. See Ray Kurzweil's February 2009 TED talk "A university for the coming singularity."

8. Marshall McLuhan, *Understanding Media: The Extension of Man*, New York: McGraw Hill, 1964.

9. See Marc de Jong and Menno van Dijk, "Disrupting beliefs: A new approach to business-model innovation," *McKinsey Quarterly*, July 2015.

10. A comment that Axel Springer has publicly repudiated as its digital recovery has gathered speed over the years; for example, in a high-profile presentation by their Head of Electronic Media, Dr. Jens Müffelmann, and Head of M&A/Strategy, Oliver Schäffer. See "Key to digitization: M&A and asset development," Axel Springer, 2012.

11. Widely cited in the Australian media; for example, Elizabeth Knight, "Media rivals facing a brave new world," *Sydney Morning Herald*, June 8, 2013.

Chapter 7. Making the right (big) moves

1. See Werner Rehm, Robert Uhlaner, and Andy West, "Taking a longer-term look at M&A value creation," *McKinsey Quarterly*, January 2012.
2. See Michael Birshan, Thomas Meakin, and Kurt Strovink, "What makes a CEO 'exceptional'?," *McKinsey Quarterly*, April 2017.
3. Though their meanings have become blurred as their popularity has grown, these are distinct concepts. The Kaizen manufacturing approach focuses on continuous improvement across sources of inefficiency in the manufacturing process, such as waste, variation, and overburden. Lean manufacturing tends to focus on the reduction of waste. See Steven Spear and H. Kent Bowen, "Decoding the DNA of the Toyota Production System," *Harvard Business Review*, September–October 1999, Vol. 77, No. 5, 96–106.
4. Six Sigma and Lean are widely used approaches to improving operational efficiency by reducing waste. Six Sigma focuses on reducing variation, while Lean attempts to remove non-value-adding steps.
5. Hasbro, Annual Company Report, 2000.
6. BASF, Annual Company Report, 2005.
7. Based on recent client work performed through Quantum Black, McKinsey's specialized big-data analytics service.
8. See "Burberry and globalisation: A checkered story," *Economist*, January 21, 2011.
9. See John Asker, Joan Farre-Mensa, and Alexander Ljungqvist, "Corporate investment and stock market listing: A puzzle?," *Review of Financial Studies*, February 1, 2015, Vol. 28, No.2. In this study they compared the investment behavior of similar public and private firms. This is one of the best studies we have seen that empirically validates the notion that stock-market listings induce short-term behavior: "We first show that private firms invest substantially more than public ones.... Second, we show that private firms' investment decisions are around four times more responsive to changes in investment opportunities than are those of public firms." See also Dominic Barton, "Capitalism for the long term," *Harvard Business Review* March 2011.
10. See Chris Bradley, Martin Hirt, and Sven Smit, "Have you tested your strategy lately?" *McKinsey Quarterly*, January 2011.

Chapter 8. Eight shifts to unlock strategy

1. See Chris Bradley, Lowell Bryan, and Sven Smit, "Managing the strategy journey," *McKinsey Quarterly*, July 2012. Our retired colleague, friend, and former leader of our Strategy Practice long pushed for this more journey-oriented approach to strategy.

2. See Lowell Bryan, "Just-in-time strategy for a turbulent world," *McKinsey Quarterly*, June 2002. Here, Bryan introduces the framework of a "portfolio of initiatives" managed across distinctly different time horizons and familiarity levels. The idea of managing growth across three horizons was developed in the McKinsey book by Baghai, Mehrdad, Stephen Coley, and David White, *The Alchemy of Growth: Practical Insights for Building the Enduring Enterprise*, Reading, MA: Perseus Books, 1999.

3. See Gary Klein, "Performing a project premortem," *Harvard Business Review*, September 2007.

4. See Fox, Bardolet, and Lieb, "Partition dependence in decision analysis, managerial decision making, and consumer choice," Chapter 10 in R. Zwick and A. Rapoport (Eds.), *Experimental Business Research*, Vol. III, Boston: Springer, 2005.

5. See Richard P. Rumelt, *Good Strategy, Bad Strategy: The Difference and Why It Matters*, New York: Crown Business, 2011. In this timeless treatise on strategy, Rumelt convinces of the importance of having a true diagnosis, focusing on choices rather than goals, driving coherency of those choices, and winding back the long-term plan to achievable proximate goals.

6. See Richard P. Rumelt, *Good Strategy, Bad Strategy: The Difference and Why It Matters*, New York: Crown Business, 2011.

Index